LAMB OF GOD

AUGUSTINE STOCK, O.S.B.

LAMB OF GOD

The Promise and Fulfillment
of Salvation

HERDER AND HERDER

1963
HERDER AND HERDER   NEW YORK
232 Madison Avenue, New York 16, N.Y.

Imprimi Potest:

> Anselm Coppersmith, O.S.B., Abbot
> October 22, 1962

Nihil Obstat:

> John R. Ready, Censor Librorum
> November 3, 1962

Imprimatur:

> Patrick C. Brennan, Vicar General,
> Diocese of Burlington
> November 6, 1962

231.7
STl

Library of Congress Catalog Card Number: 63–9554
© 1963 Herder and Herder, Inc.
Printed in the United States of America

PREFACE

Just as the mountaineer has to climb because the mountain is there, we as Christians should feel impelled to make the Scriptures our own because God willed them and inspired them. Since the Scriptures were written in a world far removed from our own, this does require effort; but the rewards are great.

Diverse as they are, the Biblical writings combine to tell the story of God's plan of salvation. St. Paul often refers to this plan as "the mystery of God"—the divine will, long hidden in God and manifested when the proper time had come, to save mankind in and through Christ Jesus. The inspired Biblical account of this plan was preceded by God's saving acts in the great events of the history of salvation; events willed and arranged according to God's eternal plan, from the Exodus to the Resurrection.

Written over a span of centuries, within the framework of varied civilizations, and using many different types of literature, God's message recorded in the Scriptures possesses a basic unity because this message shows us the one God working for the one purpose. Ideally, we should strive to see this divine work in history as one whole, from first beginning to ultimate realization. As a step toward this goal, we can concentrate our attention on various aspects of the work of salvation and try to trace out their development from first appearance to fulfillment in the Kingdom of God. This kind of study of religious ideas can never get far away from the course of historical events.

When we view God's work of salvation in its historical context, we see, among other things, how he raised a people from the condition in which he found them to the light of Christ. Sometimes modern readers are disconcerted by the negative aspects of that condition and the slowness of the change. They encounter a low moral level and a limited religious outlook in some events, strange scientific and philosophical ideas, and a way of writing history that is far removed from our modern critical standards. But it is for God to decide the time and mode of his revelation, and we must never allow ourselves to become so absorbed in these negative aspects that we neglect the unique religious splendor of the Scriptures.

It was not without some higher purpose in mind that God shows us in the inspired Scriptures this transformation of the People of God. Our efforts to relive the spirit of each succeeding stage of the history of salvation is the best preparation for an understanding of the divine message. Moreover, as Jean Levie, S.J., has pointed out recently, "this *humanistic* study of a people guided by God, of souls whom God has inspired, is worthy of its proper place in the formation of the Christian adult, at least on an equal footing with the humanistic study of the Greek and Roman mind in their pagan environment."[1]

Some of the following chapters appeared in a shorter form as articles in the *Altar and Home Pocket Missal,* and they have been expanded for the present publication with the permission of the editors of that periodical. Since this book is

1. *The Bible, Word of God in Words of Men,* New York: Kenedy, 1961, p. 211.

not intended primarily for the specialized student, all references to other Biblical studies have been kept to a minimum. It is obvious that a work such as this must rely on the labors of innumerable scholars. I am, therefore, deeply grateful to many teachers besides those whose names appear in the text.

A. S.

Contents

1.

ELECTION

The Old Testament is the literature of a whole people, the People of God, the Chosen People. They were the "chosen" people because God had elected them out of all the peoples of the earth to play a special role in his plans for the salvation of mankind. It was this divine election, in fact, and the covenant to which it gave rise, that formed the Hebrews into a people, Israel.

The Old Testament was written gradually, over a period of more than a thousand years, and it contains many different kinds of literature. Yet the Old Testament, and the Bible as a whole, possesses a basic unity. One consistent story is told. The Bible gives us the Lord's plan of salvation, the mighty works he has done in time and history for the salvation of his people Israel, and—through them—for the salvation of all mankind.

These mighty works stretch all the way from the Lord's rescue of the Hebrews from Egyptian slavery and his forming a covenant with them (Exodus-Sinai) to the establishment of the Kingdom of God in the blood of Jesus. They are proclaimed for us in the Bible in order that we may share in their fruits by our act of faith.

GOD ACTS—MEN LEARN

Running through this long history of salvation and giving unity to its thought is the theme of *divine election*. This fundamental concept with all its fruits sprang out of the events of the Exodus and the Lord's revelation of himself at Mount Sinai. Reflection on these events would later show that Yahweh had chosen Israel in unmerited grace and not because of her worth. "It was not because you were more in number than any other people that the Lord set his love upon you and chose you: for you were the fewest of all peoples. It was because he loved you" (Deut. 7:7–8). Israel's salvation was the result of God's own initiative. Yet God created man free, and he always respects that freedom. The divine initiative never reduces men to the status of puppets. The people must freely respond and accept their task within God's purpose.

God is neither capricious nor arbitrary. He is not subject to chance sympathies or antipathies and his election of Israel is not an act of arbitrariness. But it is a manifestation of his holiness and majesty which implies the right to make decisions that transcend man.

God loves and is concerned about all mankind—men are all "made in his image." Israel's election does not mean that for that reason God has rejected all the other nations. Indeed, Israel was elected only in order to serve God in the task of leading those other nations to him. In the Old Testament Israel's election is to the service of God in this world. God's choice of Israel and his "hatred" (i.e., non-choice) of other nations in no way implies their exclusion from the blessedness of the Age to Come.

Having chosen Israel, the Lord claims her for his own. The grace and deliverance, granted and accepted, laid an obligation upon Israel. The Lord's revelation of himself to this people laid upon them the obligation to conform their entire life to his nature and will. By the Exodus itself, the Lord showed that he abhors oppression and injustice. Because he is inflexibly just he hates all injustice. His people's communion with him obligates them to holy living. The Lord began to spell out the details of this obligation from the first forming of the Covenant in the Ten Commandments.

The interaction between divine election (i.e., grace and human response in faith), and the drama between privilege and responsibility, is a constant element in God's plan of salvation from the beginning up to the present. It was through their communion with the just God over the centuries that the Chosen People learned, often by their mistakes, all that this relationship implied.

Often the people thought only of the privilege and forgot the responsibility. They even *presumed* upon election, supposing that it gave them a claim on God, that God was so tied to Israel that he must stand by her even though she dishonored him. The prophets were tireless in denouncing this perversion.

The prophet Amos affirms Israel's election: "You only have I known of all the families of the earth" (3:2). To "know" in the language of the Bible implies intimacy, friendship. But this intimacy begets responsibility. Election does not give the elect the right to do with impunity what others may not do. On the contrary, this greater intimacy means that these elect must order their entire lives according to the Lord's will. So Amos goes on to say: "Therefore I will punish you for all your iniquities."

FROM MANY TO ONE

As it turned out, all of the people of Israel did not fulfill the purpose of their election. Election was not the automatic inheritance of all who were born into Israel after the flesh. The Israelites had freely to respond to God's grace at the time of the Exodus. So had each succeeding generation. The heritage of election and the privileges of the Covenant belonged to those who brought their loyalty to the Covenant and fufilled the purpose of the election. Thus it came about that the stream of election was narrowed to a Remnant, and then to one Anointed One, the elect Messiah.

During the earlier parts of their history, when they knew little of reward and punishment beyond the grave, the Israelites naturally thought of salvation or the benefits of election largely in material terms. But their national disasters and daily experience gradually convinced them that salvation must include something beyond these material benefits. In II Isaiah, of postexilic times, appears the Suffering Servant of the Lord, elect from the womb, but elect to shame and suffering for the salvation of others. "For our peace the chastisement was on him, and with his stripes we are healed" (Is. 53:5).

ELECT OF THE KINGDOM

In the Old Testament, God elected Israel in her weakness and need and delivered her. Israel freely responded to this initiative in grace and committed herself to the Lord in the Covenant which laid upon her an obligation to conform her entire life to his will. In the New Testament the same pattern is repeated, but this time on an infinitely higher level. Here God's grace and compassion are manifested for men in a need deeper than the Egyptian bondage. Here is a new deliverance by the sacrificial blood of the Lamb of God, the

Elect One (Luke 23:35), which he imparted to the elect of the Church he founded. Through that Church, he imparts this deliverance to all the nations of the world. This divine initiative demands an absolute consecration of the elect of the Kingdom of God.

God's plan of salvation, therefore, unfolds in two movements. The first, that of the Old Testament, moves from the many to the One. The other, that of the New Testament, moves from the One to the many. Between them stands the decisive salvific act: the death and resurrection of Jesus.

Throughout the Old Testament we see a process of *election* and *substitution* at work. Out of all creation man is chosen (*election*) for special communion with God ("made in God's image"), and the entire universe is in solidarity with man who is its king and perfect representative (*substitution*).

Confronted by a revelation of God, man reacted with an act of disobedience and God's curse fell on man and on all creation which is bound up with him. But love is stronger than sin. God wills to save his rebellious creation. But since man has not fulfilled his role of representation, God chooses a particular people, Israel, to hold the place of humanity (*election—substitution*).

But Israel itself is not faithful to the covenant made with God. So God must act to save again. He elects a small Remnant to take the place of the unfaithful people. But the mission of the Remnant itself will ultimately be borne by one only—the Lamb of God, *qui tollit peccata mundi,* who alone was able to both bear and take away the sins of the world.

In accordance with the principle of *election—substitution,* the history of salvation up to Christ proves to be a progressive reduction—a passage from the many to the One. God chooses mankind, Israel, the Remnant, the Elect One, substituting him for the entire created universe which alone em-

15

braces the scope of his design of love. In each of these elections God acts in time and history to save.

FROM ONE TO MANY

From Christ's death and resurrection, a victory over sin and death in death's own domain, the flesh, an inverse movement sets in. The movement now is from the One to the many, but in such a way that the many are contained in the One. Both election and salvation are "in Christ." The Church, the body of the Elect One, accomplishes the mission of the Remnant, imparting salvation to all mankind and to all creation.

In the New Testament it is St. Paul, especially, who speaks of election. God's purpose in history which operates by means of the principle of election still stands firm, says St. Paul, "based not upon men's deeds but upon the call of God" (Rom. 9:11). The most remarkable instance of that principle's working had just occurred. God had rejected Israel according to the flesh and had chosen those others who by their faith were the spiritual sons of Abraham, who by faith became the "father of many nations" (Rom. 4:17).

ELECTION AND SALVATION

St. Paul speaks of collective election—those who have faith in Christ are corporately the "elect" because they are one body in Christ, the Elect One. If they remain faithful to what they have been given, the elect will be saved in the Age to Come. But election is not predestination. "Work out your salvation in fear and trembling" St. Paul writes to the elect of the church at Philippi (2:12). And as in the Old Testament, the non-election of the Gentiles in no way implied their exclusion from the blessedness of the Age to Come, so also for the non-elect of New Testament times. Nowhere does the New Testament suggest that some individuals are predestined to a mechanical salvation and that others were created for damnation.

As in the Old Testament, election refers to God's purpose in the world—the privilege and responsibility of God's purpose as an elect instrument of his design. The measure of the privilege of this election is the measure of the task it brings, including a share in the sufferings of Jesus, the Suffering Servant. When the Lord set St. Paul apart for his special task, he said of him: "This man is a chosen instrument of mine . . . I will show him how much he must suffer for my name's sake" (Acts 9:15–16). In some degree this is true of all of the elect of God's Kingdom.

2.

COVENANT

Things had a beginning and they will have an end. This outlook is so much a part of our way of thinking that we never stop to reflect that it comes to us from divine teaching—from revelation, and especially from revelation as it is preserved in the Bible.

Creation and consummation are separated by a space of time and history—the background against which a series of events transpire. In some of these events God was directly at work (salvific acts). God was acting to save his creation. The great truths of the Bible are not timeless truths unrelated to historical circumstances. The Bible's truth is inseparably related to specific times, places, and peoples.

This preoccupation with God's acts in history, and the Lord's will, made Israel's faith a unique and radical departure from contemporary pagan religions. The latter analyzed the problem of man against *nature;* the Israelite faith analyzed the problem of life in relation to the will and purpose of God.

INFERENCE DRAWN FROM EVENTS

Israel's knowledge of God was not derived from systematic or speculative thought, but in the first instance from the events that led to the establishment of that nation, and what was learned therefrom. The people of Israel came to believe that the Lord had acted and revealed himself in the events of the Exodus and at Sinai. Belief in their *election,* that the Lord had chosen them as his special people through whom he would accomplish his saving purposes, is the chief inference drawn from this view of these historical events. If the Lord was not acting in those events, belief in their election would have been groundless.

But not all history is revelation and God's salvific acts must be distinguished from history as a whole. Revelation must be something more than human reflection on history. Israel's belief that the Lord was acting to save in the Exodus was something more than an unprovable assumption or a projection of human faith into history.

The Lord sent Israel an accredited interpreter, Moses. In the Exodus we do not have history first, followed by its interpretation, but history and interpretation in a single complex, and this can constitute real revelation. "We have first the announcement of the significant fact of the history through a prophetic person, speaking in the name of God, then the fulfilment of the announcement, and finally the interpretation of the event by one whose credentials were supplied by the fulfilment."[1]

PERSONAL AND IMPERSONAL FACTORS

The story of the deliverance in Exodus begins with a divine commission to Moses to go into Egypt to bring the people out, in the name of a God they had never known. Moses promised a deliverance he was powerless to effect.

1. H. H. Rowley, *Unity of the Bible,* New York: Living Age, 1957, p. 66.

Deliverance came not by the Israelites' own efforts but by the help of wind and wave that no man could control.

A combination of personal and impersonal factors is involved. The Exodus deliverance was not effected by Moses or entirely independent of him. "His prophetic word and the fulfilment in history dovetailed into one another, and yet neither can be explained from the other; nor did either alone provide the vehicle of the revelation."[2]

"The biblical faith is based neither on human reflection on history, nor on human claims to be the mouthpiece of God, but on both and more. For revelation through history and revelation through persons are not independent of one another, but often linked intimately together and offering a check on one another, so that while we must always speak of a faith rather than a logical demonstration, it is a faith which is intellectually respectable and for which there is solid evidence."[3]

The Lord's election of his people and the people's responsibility were given a definite form in the Covenant of Sinai.

CUTTING A COVENANT

When we enter a solemn agreement today, we draw up a written contract, which is signed, witnessed, and placed in the records. Such records did exist in the time of Moses, when the Hebrews were made the Chosen People, but the Hebrews were a desert people and had been living a nomadic life. This way of life lacked the stability that makes written

2. *Ibid.,* p. 67
3. H. H. Rowley, *Faith of Israel,* Philadelphia: Westminster, 1956, p. 21.

records practical. Among their kind of people, agreements were made by the spoken word, but the spoken word invested with ritual solemnity.

A covenant was an agreement concluded not only before human witnesses, but the gods themselves, the parties binding themselves by terrible imprecations, ritually enacted. In primitive times, covenants were sealed by swallowing a drop of each other's blood, by exchanging handclasps, or setting up pillars of stone as a memorial. The blood ritual was later refined into the practice of slaying a sacrificial animal, dismembering its body, and the parties passing between the parts. So true is this that the Israelites became accustomed to saying that the two parties had "*cut* a covenant."

The Lord gave his people a covenant. Since he is the Lord of the Universe, he cannot submit himself to obligations like men do. His covenant with the Israelites was not a parity covenant—one in which the parties bind themselves to obligations on an equal footing. The people of Moses' time also knew of another kind of covenant, the suzerainty covenant, such as a king would make with a vassal. To his vassal, the suzerain "gives" a covenant. And within the covenant the vassal finds protection and security, provided he observes the terms of the agreement. The most striking aspect in this type of covenant is the attention given to the sovereign's deeds of benevolence in favor of his vassal. The vassal's motive for obedience is that of gratitude for what has been done for him.

TERMS OF THE PACT

Hence it is that the first eighteen chapters of the book of Exodus relate all that the Lord did for his people. This is the preparation for the making of the covenant. Then Moses is commissioned to announce to the Hebrews the purpose for which Yahweh had brought them to Sinai: "Thus you shall say to the house of Jacob, and tell the people of Israel: 'You have seen for yourselves what I did to the Egyptians, and how I bore you on eagles' wings and brought you to myself. Now therefore, if you will obey my voice and keep my covenant, you shall be my own possession among all people'" (Ex. 19:4–5).

There is a condition to the agreement. The people will be the Lord's special possession if they will obey his voice. The core of the people's obligation is spelled out in the "Ten Words," the Ten Commandments (Ex. 20:1–17). These are examples of the absolute, apodictic law ("Thou shalt, Thou shalt not") that is so characteristically Hebrew.

All that remains now is to give the covenant a living reality by the blood ritual. The ceremony is described in Exodus 24. Moses built an altar at the base of Mount Sinai and set up twelve pillars, "according to the twelve tribes of Israel" (v.4.). Animals are sacrificed and half the blood is dashed against the altar, as a symbol of Yahweh's participation in the rite. The other half is put in basins, and Moses "took the book of the covenant, and read it aloud to the people; and they said, 'All that the Lord has spoken we will do, and we will be obedient.' And Moses took the blood and threw it upon the people, and said, 'Behold the blood of the covenant which the Lord has made with you in accordance with all these words'" (Ex. 34:7–8).

Spontaneously our minds leap forward to the moment when Jesus at the Last Supper took the cup in his hands and said, "this cup is the new covenant in *my* blood" (1 Cor. 11:25). Today we divide the Scriptures into the Old and the New Testament. "Testament" is just another, and less ac-

23

curate, word for "covenant." By doing so we bear witness to the vital significance of the events of the Exodus and the giving of the Covenant of Sinai.

DELIBERATE DIVINE ACT

The covenant is the basic factor in the emergence of Israel's faith and the covenant concept is perhaps the most influential in Scripture. The covenant makes it clear that the relationship between Yahweh and Israel cannot be looked upon as *natural* but placed in history by Yahweh. The pagan religions represented the relation between God and the people as a natural unity, the gods often being looked upon as the physical parents of the nations they have procreated. The covenant between Yahweh and Israel was established by a salvific act of the Lord in history.

By the covenant the Lord entered into special communion with his elect, his chosen people. The Hebrew word for covenant (*berith*) means, as it were, a circle enclosing both partners, a being brought together into an intimate relationship. Yahweh drew up the rules (Commandments) that were to pertain within the circle. Observing these rules Israel was admitted into God's sphere of life and was made holy. When Israel broke the rules they were punished but the covenant relationship was not broken.

When the people were unfaithful to the covenant they were condemned by the prophets, the conscience of Israel.[4] But the prophets were prophets of salvation as well as prophets of judgment and punishment. God's covenant,

4. Cf. B. Vawter, C.M., *Conscience of Israel,* New York: Sheed and Ward, 1961, pp. 16 f.

which had been brought into being by him, would also be restored by him. A Remnant would survive.

SHAPES CULT AND ETHICS

The covenant relationship shaped nearly every aspect of Israel's life. Israelite worship and liturgy (cult), for example, must be viewed against the background of the doctrine of the holiness of God, the sinfulness of man, and covenant between this holy God and this sinful man. Again and again people and individuals were in danger of breaking the communion established between God and man by the covenant. This gives Israelite worship a permanent tendency to *atonement,* to maintain and restore this communion on both the communal and the individual plane.

Intercourse between man and man (ethics) was put on a new plane by the covenant. Admitted into communion with the holy God, the people must also be holy: "you shall be to me a kingdom of priests and a holy nation" (Ex. 19:6). Promulgating the Commandments as the rules of the covenant, the Lord gave moral law a religious nature. In the Code of Holiness of the book of Leviticus (cc. 17–26) again and again the injunction is repeated: "You shall be holy; for I the LORD your God am holy." Nearly all of its moral injunctions end with the words: "I am the LORD." In other words, this commandment is transmitted and known in a religious connection.

In addition to the ties of common ancestry and experience and whatever else bound them together as a people, the chosen people were united by the covenant bond, which in its original context was probably looked upon as an extension of blood-relationship. Ideally others were looked upon as brothers rather than compatriots and every bargain was a matter of covenant, of personal relations, rather than contract.

COVENANT RENEWAL

After the people of Israel entered into Palestine, the covenant continued to shape their lives. Chapter 24 of the book of Joshua describes a great convocation held at Shechem, the ancient Canaanite fortress and religious center. In the presence of the assembled Israelite tribes and their leaders, Joshua reviews all the Lord's great deeds in their behalf, beginning with the patriarchal period and dwelling especially on the events of the Exodus and the conquests in Transjordan and the Canaanite hill country. On the basis of this summary Joshua demands a decision on Israel's part. "Now therefore fear the LORD, and serve him in sincerity and in faithfulness; put away the gods which your fathers served beyond the River (Euphrates), and in Egypt, and serve the LORD. And if you be unwilling to serve the LORD, choose this day whom you will serve, whether the gods your fathers served in the region beyond the River, or the gods of the Amorites (Canaanites) in whose land you dwell" (Joshua 24:14–15).

The Lord has a way of reminding them of their covenant fidelity, or their lack of it. "He is a jealous God; he will not forgive your transgressions or your sins. If you forsake Yahweh and serve foreign gods, then he will turn and do you harm, and annihilate you, after having done you good" (v. 19–20). The people choose for the Lord: "The LORD our

God we will serve, and his voice we will obey" (v. 24). The convocation ends again with the giving of laws, and a ritual enactment of the agreement entered into.

"So Joshua made a covenant for the people that day, and made statutes and ordinances for them at Shechem. And Joshua wrote these words in the book of the law of God; and he took a great stone, and set it up there under the oak in the sanctuary of the LORD. And Joshua said to all the people, 'Behold, this stone shall be a witness against us; for it has heard all the words of the LORD which he spoke to us; therefore it shall be a witness against you, to keep you from denying your God' " (v. 26–27). Joshua's covenant renewal seems to have embraced some tribes that had not been party to the original covenant.

COVENANT OR CULTURE

But when Joshua died "another generation succeeded him who did not know the LORD or what he had done for Israel" (Judges 2:10). Once the Israelites had settled in Canaan and become an agricultural people a struggle between their faith in Yahweh and pagan nature religion began that was to continue until it was resolved in the downfall of the nation. In the Exodus and in the desert the Lord had shown that he was master of wind and wave and could disrupt the established order. But could he also provide wine, and oil, and grain—maintain the established order and insure the fertility of the land as the nature religions claimed they could?

The battle raged back and forth. According to the book of Judges, the religious observance of the Israelites during that period followed a regular pattern of infidelity, punishment, repentance, and mercy shown. "The people of Israel did what was evil in the sight of the LORD and served the Baals. . . . So the anger of the LORD was kindled against Israel, and he gave them over to plunderers. . . . Then the LORD raised up judges who saved them out of the power of those who plundered them" (Judges 2:11, 14, 16).

Now and again the Old Testament writings give us a glimpse of that centuries-long struggle. Such is the fierce clash between the prophet Elijah and Jezebel, King Ahab's Phoenician queen (1 Kings 17–19, 21). Another prophet, Hosea, likens Israel to Gomer, his own unfaithful wife:

> *For she said, "I wish to run after my lovers,*
> *they give me my bread and my water,*
> *my wool and my flax, my oil and my drink."*
> *Hosea 2:7*

DEUTERONOMIC REFORM

After the ten northern tribes had been swept from the board, in the time of King Josiah of Judah, a copy of the Law (probably Deuteronomy 12–26) was found in the Temple, 622 B.C. King Josiah uses it to renew the covenant. "And the king went up to the temple of the LORD, and with him all the men of Judah and all the inhabitants of Jerusalem, and the priests and the prophets, all the people, both small and great; and he read in their hearing all the words of the book of the covenant which had been found in the temple of the LORD. And the king stood by the pillar and made a covenant before the LORD, to walk after the LORD and to keep his commandments and his testimonies and his statutes, with all his heart and all his soul, to perform the words of this covenant that were written in this book; and all the people joined in the covenant" (2 Kings 23:2–3). Afterwards King Josiah cleansed his kingdom of the trappings of Baal worship. The incident makes it clear to us how close the covenant came to disappearing altogether.

But the Deuteronomic reform came too late to save the people from doom. It was this sad message that the prophet Jeremiah was commissioned to impart. Jerusalem will fall to the Babylonians. But the word of Yahweh was renewal and promise as well as judgment and doom. It builds and plants as well as wrecks and ruins. Once the false foundations had been swept aside, the Lord would build anew. A New Covenant, a New People, and a New Age lay on the other side of catastrophe.

"Behold, the days are coming, says the LORD, when I will make a New Covenant with the house of Israel and the house of Judah, not like the covenant which I made with their fathers. . . . I will put my law within them, and I will write it upon their hearts. Then I will be their God, and they shall be my people" (31:31–33).

NEW COVENANT

Evidently this prophecy made a deeper impression on later tradition than anything else Jeremiah said. Again we are reminded at once of Jesus' words "this cup is the *New Covenant* in my blood" (1 Cor. 11:25). That it became the name for the canon of Christian writings (New Testament means

New Covenant) is singularly striking evidence of Jesus' role in the plan of salvation.

The words "Behold, the days are coming" indicate that this prophecy has to do with "the last things" (eschatology), the consummation of the divine purpose in history. While it will possess an efficacy of a higher order than the old, the New Covenant will fulfill the original intention of the Sinai covenant.

Putting the finishing touches to the Pentateuch in the post-exilic period, the priestly writer regards all history from the point of view of the covenant. From his position within the worshipping community of Israel he looks back across the patriarchal and primeval periods to the very beginning, the creation. From this point of view, he presents God's revelation as unfolding according to a prearranged plan in four successive eras, each marked by the dispensing of certain privileges and duties: creation, covenant with Noah, covenant with Abraham, covenant at Sinai.

Ezra the priest brought with him from Babylonia a copy of this Law, edited by priestly writers during the captivity, and made it the basis of the postexilic community. We find him using it to lead the people in a covenant renewal that is strikingly similar to the covenant ceremony of Josiah's time (Nehemiah 8–9).

NEW MOSES

In various places and ways the New Testament affirms the essence of its message: Jesus of Nazareth has fulfilled the promise contained in the old covenant, bringing a salvation whose excellence had been only suggested when God began

30

his work in history 1,200 years before in the person of Moses.

One way that the New Testament affirms this is to present Jesus as the New Moses. Moses had been the mediator of the old covenant; so Jesus was the mediator of the New. "For there is one God, and also one mediator between God and man, Christ Jesus, himself man, who gave himself as a ransom for all" (1 Tim. 2:5). St. Paul writes to the Galatians (3:19), that the old covenant was "ordained by angels through a mediator." The implication is that there is now no need for a human mediator, since we have direct access to God in Christ. "A mediator is not needed for one party acting alone, and God is one" (v. 20).

The epistle to the Hebrews, especially, portrays Christ as the mediator of the New Covenant. In Jewish thought the high priest was the mediator after the death of Moses and Hebrews is the only New Testament book that explicitly calls Jesus "priest" or "high priest." Christ is the mediator of a new or better covenant: "Christ has obtained a ministry which is as much more excellent than the old as the covenant he mediates is better" (Heb. 8:6). Indeed, Hebrews goes on to quote the passage from Jeremiah (31:31–34) in which the prophet foretold the formation of a New Covenant and affirms its realization in the blood of Jesus (31:31–34).

The better we understand the Scriptures the more meaningful become Jesus' words at the last supper: "This cup is the New Covenant in my blood" (Luke 22:20). We can never grasp the meaning of his mission and person apart from them.

3.

PEOPLE OF GOD

The Israelites, the Chosen People, were the people of God. By a varied combination of forces and circumstances, groups of humans become banded together and marked off from mankind in general. There are many peoples in the world today—American, Mexican, Italian, Greek. The forces and circumstances that go to make a people a people are themselves bewilderingly complex. But in the case of the people of God, they are even more so. They became a people for no apparent reason—the ordinary forces and circumstances do not seem to have been at work. And they not only became a people—they became the people of God.

A group may have distinctive historical existence and become the subject of a history under one of three headings: as a *race,* as a *nation,* or as a *people.*[1] Race is essentially a biological designation, following from common ancestry. Nation is a political designation, implying the unity of centralized government. It is more difficult to pin down the essence of "peoplehood."

In any case, it is fairly obvious that Israel did not owe her historical existence to the fact that she was either race or nation. As far as race is concerned, Israel was mixture of racial strains from the beginning and in no essential distinct from

1. Cf. J. Bright, *Early Israel in Recent History Writing,* Chicago: Allenson, 1956, p. 113.

her neighbors. The book of Exodus states that when the Hebrews left Egypt they were a mixed group: not only descendants of Jacob but "a mixed multitude" (12:38) representing Semites of various origins.

Nor did the Israelites become a distinctive group by the fact that they were a nation. Israel was a nation but for a relatively brief period (1000–586 B.C.). A history of Israel cannot be restricted to any form of government under which she lived.

A PEOPLE BY FAITH

So Israel became a distinctive group of humans only as a "people." But as we have said, the forces and circumstances that make a group of people are bewilderingly complex. To be a "people" is to be bound together in a cultural unity, but the bonds that create such units are extremely varied. Cultural units "may be created by common language, common religion, common historical experience, common commercial interests—or any combination of all, or some of these factors, and others besides."[2] To determine what makes a people a people we must look for those factors that draw it together into a cultural unit and set it apart from all other units.

What was it then that made Israel Israel? What set her apart from her neighbors? Israel did not owe her historical existence to the fact that she was either race or nation: this we have seen. Nor was it language, habitat, historical experience, nor material culture that made Israel Israel—but faith. And since faith is the reason for their "peoplehood,"

2. *Ibid.*, p. 114.

the Israelites become not only a people but the people of God.

The Israelites began to exist as a people as consequence of the Lord's will to impart salvation to mankind. To carry out this salvific will, the Lord elected a people through whom he would work. But he did not elect one of the great peoples or nations already existing. He chose a helpless band of slaves living in Egypt. His liberating them (the Exodus) was the decisive event that made these Hebrews into the people Israel. At Sinai the Lord invites them to enter into a covenant with him, to freely decide to become the people of God. "If you will obey my voice and keep my covenant, you shall be my own possession among all peoples; for all the earth is mine, and you shall be to me a kingdom of priests and a holy nation" (Ex. 19:5–6). God has elected Israel, made a covenant with her, formed her into a people, but because he has a concern "for all the earth." This people is to be his instrument of salvation.

RELIGIOUS COMMUNITY

By their very origin, therefore, the people of God existed only through and for their God. For them to live on a merely human level, to seek human goods by merely human means, is to fall short of their vocation.

From the outset Israel was a religious community rather than a nation whose unity resulted from natural forces. A reflection of this is that all the collections of traditions depict Moses as a *prophetic* figure rather than a national hero or a military leader. The historians regard Israel's struggle as a holy war, their "sacrificial ban" (*cherem*) as a sacred act.

The Lord is savior and God of the covenant from the origin of his people. United with his people in the communion of the covenant, the Lord proved his fidelity again and again. This gave Israel's faith its unique warmth and profound consciousness of mercy and fidelity.

The type of government under which the people of God lived during the period of the judges emphasized the nature of their "peoplehood" and protected them from perversions. Unlike all other peoples of their time, the people of God had no king. Thus they were vividly reminded that faith in Yahweh and their own peoplehood went hand in hand. Occasionally the Lord intervened in their behalf through judges and seers to whom he granted his spirit. And year after year the people gathered at the tribal sanctuary to renew their covenant with the Lord.

PEOPLE AT WAR

But this people, set apart and sanctified, will not be held apart forever from all contact with other peoples. And since the other peoples were given up to idolatry and abominations, the people of God will have to resist them with the strength of their Lord. They will be a people at war. They knew from their beginning as a people that the history of the world is determined by a great combat against the forces of evil, a combat in which they are necessarily engaged by their engagement with God, and in which they must act only in faith.[3]

3. Cf. J. Giblet, et al., *The God of Israel, the God of Christians*, New York: Desclée, 1961, p. 48 f.

Under the Philistine threat, the loose tribal confederacy of the time of judges gave way to kingship; Israel became "like the nations." The Lord assigned an important role to the house of David in his plans of salvation. Yet the introduction of monarchy into Israel was followed by many evils. Their society was radically secularized and they knew the temptations of material success. They thought to succeed humanly, often to the neglect of their Lord's will.

The Israelites owed their existence as a people, and as the people of God, to the Lord's election, which had called for a response of faith and a holy life. But then many came to feel that the privileges were theirs by physical descent from the line of the patriarchs alone. The Lord sent his prophets to recall the demands and beauties of the covenant and threaten the punishments of infidelity. The prophet Hosea upbraids Israel for infidelity; he names two of his children Lo-Rouchama (Not Pitied) and Lo-Ammi (Not My People). But even the punishments that came do not mark a definitive rupture. They are rather the sign of the Lord's attentive fidelity and exigent love. A "remnant" will perdure in increased fidelity; in them the promises will be fulfilled. One is a member of the true people of God only by a humble, active fidelity.

Israel is God's people and God is a God of life, who remains faithful to all eternity. The Israel of the time of the prophets must perish, but God will raise a new people from the remnant that will be saved.

KINGDOM OF PRIESTS

In the same direction as the message of the prophets is the word of the Deuteronomic authors, who left their imprint on historical books from Genesis to 2 Kings. Their aim was to lead Israel back to the fulfillment of her calling as the chosen people of God. The people's obedience must reveal itself not only in pure worship but in circumcision of the heart—the observance of his commandments. Election must find acknowledgement in responsibility, otherwise it brings judgment. The Deuteronomic viewpoint seems to have left its imprint on the wording of the injunction to holy living, the terms of the Sinai covenant: "You shall be to me a kingdom of priests and a holy nation" (Ex. 19:6).

The prophet Jeremiah saw that King Josiah's reform came too late to stave off punishment. Jerusalem must fall, but beyond disaster he foresaw salvation. A New Covenant will be given, establishing a New People.

The demand for holiness on the people's part reaches it fruition during and after the exile. Stripped of kingdom and temple after the destruction of Jerusalem, the people of God were again organized *religiously* under the direction of priests and scribes. That the people of God could survive this and other unprecedented disasters is clear evidence that the original cohesive force had been religious.

WORSHIPPING COMMUNITY

Paradoxically, the sense of belonging to the covenant community was intensified, rather than weakened, by life under captivity. The people devoted themselves to the study of their sacred traditions and to the task of preserving them in writing for future generations. Jerusalem fallen, they had to find a new understanding of the community that still bound them together despite national disaster. Searching their traditions, they were reminded that the covenant community originated at a time when Israel was not a nation and had no king, except Yahweh himself.

The Deuteronomic editor had taken for granted that the covenant community would be organized politically as a *kingdom,* ideally united under a king of the family of David. During the first years of the exile, however, Ezekiel, a Jerusalem priest, advocated a different view of the covenant community. While leaving room for a "prince" (44:3), Ezekiel believed that fundamentally Israel would be a "kingdom of priests" (Ex. 19:6), a worshipping community, a *qahal*—a word which one day was to be translated into Greek by *ekklesia* and thence into English as "church." The *qahal* is the assembly of the people united about their religious and civil leaders, for divine worship.

This view of the people of God was further developed by members of the priestly order who were carried into exile. The priestly traditions, the last strand of the Pentateuch, was edited in their circle and bears the imprint of their viewpoint.

SIGN AMONG NATIONS

Israel was called (*election*) to be a holy community, set apart from all other nations in order that the holy God might take up his "tabernacle" in her midst. "I will dwell in the midst of the people of Israel forever. And the house of Israel shall no more defile my holy name" (Ezek. 43:7). To keep the people of God separate (and thereby holy, it was hoped) the priestly tradition laid great emphasis on rites and prescriptions that marked Israel as the people of God (circumcision, feasts, "kosher" or permitted foods).

The Lord is the Holy One and he manifests his holiness by

sanctifying the people that he has chosen, adapting them to himself, acting with power and goodness in their favor. The people of God must correspond to the Lord's dynamic holiness in the midst of a sinful world. "You shall not profane my holy name, that I may be hallowed among the people of Israel; I am the LORD who sanctify you, who brought you out of the land of Egypt to be your God" (Lev. 22:32–33).

This people must be like a sign among the nations, a witness people, a mediator people. It is by seeing them that the nations learn to know the one true God. A "kingdom of priests," consecrated to the worship and service of the Lord, their worship will include a liturgy and a specialized priesthood. But it will by no means be limited to this. Men serve the infinitely good and just God only by loving him and conforming themselves to his will. Rightly, worship cannot be separated from a holy, moral life.

As the Levites were set apart as a priesthood within Israel, so Israel as a people was set apart as a priesthood to the world. Looking forward to the day when the covenant promise would be realized, the prophet Zechariah wrote: "In those days, ten men, from nations of every tongue, shall take hold of the robe of a Jew, saying, 'Let us go with you, for we have heard that God is with you' " (8:23).

While some circles entrench themselves in particularism and stubborn nationalism, the "poor of the Lord" long for the coming of the One Who Is Sent, the Messiah, who will establish the New People of God.

GOD'S OWN PEOPLE

The New Testament's affirmation regarding God's plan of salvation from the point of view of this particular concept, the people of God, is clear-cut: the mixed Christian community of Jews and Gentiles is the New People of God.

The new covenant made by the shedding of the blood of Jesus Christ has created a new people of God. Reflecting on the entrance of the Gentiles into the Kingdom, St. Paul recalls Hosea's symbolic gesture of naming his children Lo-Rouchama (Not Pitied) and Lo-Ammi (Not My People). But in the time of salvation beyond punishment, said Hosea, the Lord will say: "I will have pity on Lo-Rouchama; I will say to Lo-Ammi, 'You are my people,' and he shall say, 'My God!' " (2:25). This has been fulfilled in an unexpected manner in the entrance of the Gentiles into the Kingdom *before* Israel. "Even us whom he has called, not from the Jews only but also from the Gentiles, as indeed he says in Hosea, 'Those who were not my people I will call *My People,* and her who was not beloved, I will call My Beloved' " (Rom. 9:25).

Thinking of the new people of the new covenant that Jesus has formed for himself, St. Paul instinctively reverts to the Sinai covenant and its demand for holiness on the people's part. In words that reflect Ex. 19:5, St. Paul writes to Titus that "our great God and Savior, the Christ Jesus . . . gave himself for us to redeem us from all iniquity and *to purify for himself a people of his own"* (2:13–14).

And this is also the case with St. Peter. In a most striking affirmation that the *church* is the true people of God, he writes to Christians of his time: "But you, you are a *chosen race, a royal priesthood, a holy nation,* God's own people, that you may declare the wonderful deeds of him who called you out of darkness into his marvelous light. Once *you were no people* but now you are God's people; once *you had not received mercy* but now *you have received mercy"* (1 Peter 2:9–10). On a new level of excellence, election and covenant again bring in privilege and responsibility.

4.

CREATION

Revelation by God rather than speculation by man is the keynote of the Bible. The Hebrews lacked the kind of intellectual curiosity that made Greek philosophy possible. Israel's belief in God did not originate from reflections on the nature of things. It was not the achievement of the philosopher arguing back to the first cause. Israel derived its knowledge of God, not from nature, but from the acts of God in the history of his people, as they appeared in the light of his revelation to Moses and the prophets.

God the Creator occupies a less important place than God the Savior; the maker of heaven and earth a less important place than the Lord who led his people out of Egypt. It was through the prophetic realization that God is the Lord of history that there came about the recognition of God as the Creator of the universe.

We may get the opposite impression if we begin to read the Bible with the book of Genesis. But the creation stories of Genesis are a preface and like most prefaces were written after the main portion of the work was completed.

SALVATION BEFORE CREATION

Without a doubt, Israel honored its God as Creator, as did the other ancient oriental peoples. Each and every religion considers its god to be the creator. Belief in the creation must have existed as an integral element in the idea of the one, true God. And this must have been the case from the earliest times. When Israel's belief in creation was explicitly formulated, it immediately showed a character of its own, distinguishing it from pagan notions of creation.

Belief in God as Creator is apparent in the older parts of the Old Testament, in the historical and prophetic books, for example, but seldom does it come to the fore. It is only in Jeremiah and particularly in the prophecies of II Isaiah that God is proclaimed as Creator.

CREATION MYTHS

During the days of those prophets, the struggle between the kingdom of Israel and the empires of Assyria and Babylonia reached its tragic conclusion. These Mesopotamian cultures had highly developed creation myths, embodying ideas and principles that could not be reconciled with faith in the Lord. It is not unlikely that the explicit Israelite doctrine of creation was elaborated as an answer to this pagan Mesopotamian philosophy of life.

Regarding the Israelite world-picture, we must be prepared to admit that is impossible to reduce Israelite ideas about the make-up of the world to a single type. Even if they had a coherent system, it is certain that we know of it only by allusions. And, moreover, scientific interest, as we understand it today, was outside the concern of the Biblical writers.

Yet it is safe to say that the Israelite world-picture did not differ essentially from that of the other ancient oriental peoples. They conceived of the world as a sort of three-storey building, the heavens above, the earth below, and the waters under the earth. The earth was a plane, surrounded by the ocean, resting on the waters below, covered by the dome-like starry sky.

The sky was thought of as a solid construction, a "firmament," resting upon pillars, forming the dome of the earth. This solid heavenly vault separated the terrestrial ocean from the celestial. Its rupture would be equivalent to a return to primeval chaos. Above this dome the ocean of heaven was thought to lie, and above that the heaven of heavens, where God has established his throne, Psalm 104 (103):3. The columns supporting the vault seem to have been identical with the mountains. The roots of these same mountains, going down into the waters of the subterranean ocean, supported the flat surface of the earth.[1]

RELIGIOUS AFFIRMATION

In their world-picture, then, the Israelites shared the ideas common to the ancient world. It is very clear that this world-picture was not an element of revelation in the Old Testament and it would be pointless to attempt to defend it against modern scientific conceptions. *The Scripture's real teaching lies elsewhere.* Israel came to see that this world had been created by the one, holy, and loving God, and applied its belief in the God of salvation and grace to the ancient nations of the world. In this way Israel arrived at a distinctive description of the world's creation.

Ancient Israel knew one or perhaps several creation myths

1. Cf. E. Jacob, *Theology of the Old Testament,* London: Hodder and Stoughton, 1958, pp. 145 f.

which it shared with neighboring peoples. The word "myth" as used here has a special meaning. For the ancient peoples a myth was definitely more than a fictitious story. For the pagan peoples surrounding Israel, the objects of the external world and human acts were real and of value only insofar as they reproduced and repeated a primordial act, an act that had been previously performed by a divine being.[2]

A myth is an account that has the power to reactualize, *to bring back,* tremendous events that occurred at the beginning of time. Myth and liturgical ritual were very closely related, acts of cult being often nothing other than dramatic representations of the events described in the myth.

RITUAL MYTHS

When the pagan peoples told their creation myths or dramatized them in their life of worship, they believed that they reactualized the events that occurred at the beginning of time, at the origins of the world and of mankind.

The creation myths of the various pagan peoples surrounding the Holy Land were essentially alike. The names of the gods and details of the myth may have varied from people to people, but the myth was essentially one. The creation account of the book of Genesis is an almost point by point refutation of these pagan concepts.

Typically the pagan myth tells how the gods emerged from some pre-existing element; the sea, for example. A primordial struggle took place between a god of Order (and fertility) and a god of Chaos, who was commonly connected with the

2. Cf. M. Eliade, *Cosmos and History,* New York: Harper Torchbooks, 1954, pp. 3–6.

sea. The god of Chaos was overcome and slain, and the world was formed from his body. Later the fertility god's power was disputed by a god of summer drought. The god of fertility was slain and carried down to the underworld. Then, through the assistance of a female deity, who had been seized by a great passion for him, the god of fertility escaped from the underworld and the lovers were united.

NATURE RELIGIONS

These various deities were identified with the powers of nature, fertility, summer drought, and the like. Nor is the struggle between the deities a struggle that took place once for all at the beginning of time. It is waged in nature, year by year, as the seasons come and go. And man was not a mere spectator of this conflict. By telling the myth and dramatizing it in their liturgy, the ancient pagans thought that they could insure the victory of the god of fertility and his union with his consort, which in turn would insure fertility for the land for the coming year.

Israel, we have seen, knew several creation myths. This is to be detected less in the creation accounts of the book of Genesis than in certain passages of the prophets and poetic books, which speak of the Lord's crushing the power of sea monsters such as Rahab and Leviathan.

> *By his power he calmed the sea;*
>   *by his understanding he smote Rahab.*
>
> *Job 26:12*

> *Awake, awake, put on strength,*
>   *O arm of the LORD;*

awake, as in days of old,
    the generations of long ago.
Was it not thou that didst cut Rahab in pieces,
    that didst pierce the dragon?

                                        Isaiah 51:9

Yet, O God, my King from of old,
    working saving deeds in the midst of the earth.
You divided the sea by your might;
    you smashed the heads of the dragons on the waters.
You crushed the heads of Leviathan,
    you gave him as food for
    the creatures of the wilderness.

                                        Psalm 74(73):12–14

Yet it is clear that these references to pagan myths are nothing more than literary allusions. It was much the same as a Christian making a literary allusion to Greek mythology with no thought of adopting paganism as a religious faith.

LITERARY ALLUSIONS

But in the creation accounts of Genesis, we have more than literary allusions. These accounts and their poetic parallel in Psalm 104(103), which are the only passages where theological reflection about creation is exercised, expose the fallacies of the pagan outlook, point by point. The two accounts (Gen. 1:1–2:4a and 2:4b–25) come from different ages and backgrounds and, viewed as world-pictures, they are incompatible with each other and with modern science. But in the essential religious teaching they are the same.

The one true God did not evolve from any previously existing material nor is he identified with any power of nature. Before he created the world, he was, and his "Spirit was moving over the face of the waters." He created all things, nor did he have to struggle with a hostile power to bring them into existence. "God said: 'Let there be light; and there was light.'" Woman is not a sub-human object of pleasure but the essential equal of man: she was formed from his rib.

These creation accounts are clearly not myths in the sense explained. The essential elements are missing, such as the generation of gods and struggle between them, and repetition of the account. Among the pagans, creation remained limited to the domain of myth and ritual and was thus imprisoned in an ever-recurring cycle of seasons. The world of the gods and the world of historical reality remained closed to each other.

COLORED BY COVENANT COMMUNION

But in Israel creation marks a commencement. It is the starting point for a real movement in history. The phrase "in the beginning" in the first verse of Genesis designates a whole plan of action. It shows us that God's plan in history has creation as its starting point. The word "generations" (*toledot*) is used for both the creation of the world and the genealogy of the patriarchs, and Jews still express this unity of creation and history by dating their calendar from the creation of the world.

But, as we have seen already, Israel's belief in God did not arise from abstract reflections on the nature of things but from revelation—from the acts of God in the history of his people as they appeared in the light of revelation. In Scripture the idea of creation was far more on the periphery than the historical experience of salvation.

Israel took up the question of creation explicitly only after it had experienced the Lord's salvation. What the Scriptures have to say about creation is colored by that experience. Israel applied its belief in the God of salvation and grace to an ancient conception of the world and this shaped the Old Testament and New Testament conceptions of the world.

DUALISM EXCLUDED

"This made it possible to see nature as an entity, to know the world as the perfect work of God, to recognize a close relationship between God and the world. Considered in this light the world can never be a power hostile to man, the natural gifts and powers in this world can never be condemned in themselves. There can be no sin in the nature of things as such, but only in the will of man. This cuts off every tragic outlook upon life, every tragic way of thought, at the root. This dogma also opens up the possibility of viewing suffering in this world from the aspect of guilt (Gen. 2 f.), thus overcoming fundamentally all dualism and demonism. This linking together of Israel's faith in the God of Salvation and the Creation of the world gives to the Old Testament philosophy of life a clarity, tranquility, warmth, and grandeur not to be found outside the Bible."[3]

The revelation of the Lord of salvation and mercy, starting with the exodus from Egypt and the covenant of Sinai, stands at the core of the Old Testament. The creation accounts were later added as a preface. Consequently, as the Bible presents

3. C. Vriezen, *Outline of Old Testament Theology*, Boston: Branford, 1958, p. 186.

it, creation is directed toward the covenant. Why did God create the world? The Old Testament answers: for the covenant, for the Lord's plan of life and salvation given to all humanity by means of Israel.

BOTH DIRECTIONS FROM COVENANT

Putting the finishing touches to the Pentateuch in the post-exilic period, the priest editor regarded all history from the point of view of the covenant. Looking back across the patriarchal and primeval periods to the very beginning, to creation, he presents God's revelation as unfolding according to a prearranged plan found in successive covenants: covenant of creation, with Noah, with Abraham, at Sinai. Clearly the creation accounts that head this series belong not in the sphere of natural science but in that of the history of mankind's salvation.

And as we can look backwards from the covenant to creation so we can look forward to salvation, the full realization of the Lord's will to save—a New Creation.

Because of sin, mankind and the world did not succeed in keeping the perfection they possessed at the time of their creation. By his disobedience to the divine command, man lost his proper place in God's creation. Because this is so, all creation is out of kilter in a sense and groans for redemption.

BASIS OF SALVATION

But judgment was not the Lord's final word. He begins to act to save his creation. Election and covenant form a people of God, the Lord's instrument of salvation. The covenant is the foundation-stone of the expectation of salvation. Being a faithful God, the Lord could never forsake Israel entirely but will use her to carry out his saving will. This is true even if, as the prophets warned, only a remnant would remain to be a partner in the New Covenant.

Jeremiah foretells the destruction of Jerusalem but beyond catastrophe he sees the establishment of a New Covenant and a New People. And since the Sinai covenant had become connected with creation by retrojection, it follows that the New Covenant should be associated with a New Creation. In the earlier strata of the Old Testament, salvation means simply deliverance from national disaster and physical perils. But more and more salvation became associated with the great deliverance from Egypt at the Red Sea. When the whole of creation came to be viewed from the point of view of the covenant, the original act of creation was regarded as a great divine act of salvation. This extension of meaning was all the easier since the primitive creation myths spoke of a god of order overcoming a god of disorder. Psalm 74 (73), we have suggested, is a negative print of this concept.

NEW EXODUS

When the prophets looked to acts of salvation that lay in the future, they instinctively described them in terms of the great act of salvation of the past, the Exodus. Return from the Babylonian exile was to be a New Exodus.

"I am the LORD, your Holy one,
the Creator of Israel, your King."

52

Thus says the LORD,
  who makes a way in the sea,
  a path in the mighty waters, . . .
Behold, I am doing a new thing,
  it springs forth, already do you not perceive it?
I will make a way in the wilderness
  and rivers in the desert.

                               Isaiah 43:15–16, 19

NEW CREATION

The New Testament proclaims the good news of salvation. The awaited great act of salvation and the new creation has already taken place in the death and resurrection of Jesus Christ. The new creation, the Kingdom of God, is a present reality; a divine reality inaugurated in the present age as it were by anticipation. "If anyone is in Christ, he is a new creation" (2 Cor. 5:17). Yet it looks for its perfect realization and revelation when the Lord will return to judge.

St. Paul often represents the work of Jesus as the creation of a new humanity, one which the faithful "put on" like a robe at baptism, when they "put away" their old, fallen human nature. The Kingdom, as a visible society into which men enter, is dynamic, a present reality that grows until the time of final consummation. The Kingdom as it exists in the souls of the faithful (grace) is also dynamic. The Christian has put on the new humanity but he must continue to grow in it until he reaches the full stature of Christ. Thus St. Paul writes to the Ephesians: "You must give up your former manner of life and put off the old man . . . and put on the New Man, created after the likeness of God in justice and holiness of the truth" (4:23–24). Faith is both a gift and a task.

A new Genesis has taken place in Jesus Christ. In the new humanity, which is the new creation of God in Jesus Christ, the divisions created by sin in the old creation are abolished. God has created "one new man" (Eph. 2:15) so that all humanity can now be as one, Jew and Greek, male and female. "All of you, baptized into Christ, have put on Christ. There is neither Jew nor Greek, slave nor free man, male nor female; for you are all one in Christ Jesus" (Gal. 3:27–28). From the beginning baptism has been universal in a sense that circumcision could never be.

REDEMPTION OF CREATION

Because man lost his proper place in God's creation through sin, the old creation as a whole was injured and groaned for redemption. Through God's New Creation in Christ, by making it possible for mankind to reoccupy its proper place in the scheme of things, the original unity and harmony is being restored. "For creation waits with eager expectation for the revealing of the sons of God. . . . We know it well enough—the whole created universe has been groaning in all its parts as if in the pangs of childbirth up to the present. And not only creation: we ourselves, who have the first fruits of the Spirit, groan inwardly as we wait for adoption as sons, the redemption of our bodies" (Rom. 8:19, 22–23).

Finally, in the New Testament, we see reflected the conviction to which the Church was brought. This same Jesus is not only the Lord of salvation but is himself divine, the eternal Word, the Lord of the cosmos.

> *He is the Image of the invisible God,*
> *First-Born of all creation,*
> *for in him all things were created,*
> *in heaven and on earth*
> *visible and invisible,*
> *Thrones, Dominions, Principalities, Powers;*
> *He is before all things, and in him all things hold*
> *together.*
>
> *Col. 1:16–17*

5.

SIN

The notion that people have about sin depends very much on the notion they have about God. Sin always presupposes God and his law, so that a person's conception of God determines what he thinks about sin. The idea of sin follows the idea of God.

Because of God's special dealings with Israel, their idea of God, and therefore of sin, became *distinctive,* unlike that of any other people. Their belief in God did not originate from philosophical speculation, or reflections on the nature of things. Israel derived its knowledge of God from experience —from experiencing the acts of God in their history. This intervention was explained to them by God through Moses and the prophets.

In revealing himself to his people, the Lord not only revealed the fact that he *exists,* but, what is actually more important, he revealed his *character, what kind of a God he is.* Belief in the existence of God is common to a number of religions, however that belief may have been arrived at. But what do they think God is like? This is where they differ: in their conception of the nature and character of God.

THE MORAL GOD

Now from the very beginning of God's special dealings with his people Israel, by the things that he did, the Lord began to manifest his nature and character to his people. The Lord elected his people and delivered them from Egyptian slavery. The Lord did this out of compassion for Israel. *"I have seen, I have seen the affliction of my people who are in Egypt. I have heard their cry under their overseers; I know their sufferings, and I have come down to deliver them out of the hand of the Egyptians"* (*Ex. 3:7–8*).

In the very acts that established Israel as a people, the essential elements of God's character were revealed. The events of the Exodus and the making of the covenant already contained the seeds of a teaching about God that is everlastingly true.

In these two events God revealed himself to Israel as *personal, active in history,* and the *master of nature*. But above all, Israel came to see that God's activity was governed by a moral purpose. This is not to say that there was a moral law to which the Lord himself was subject. Rather, it is to say that the Lord is himself *a moral being* and that the moral law was itself unfolded in his freeing Israel from Egypt and in making the covenant.

ETHICAL RELIGION

Most religions predicated a moral code for their followers but more often than not the gods themselves were exempt from the code. The religion of the Old Testament recognized from the beginning, and with increasing clarity as time passed, that the Lord is moral by his very nature. Israel saw that what God is, they who worship him must become. The religion of the Old and the New Testament is ethical by its very nature.

When the Lord made the covenant with his elected people,

the condition he laid down was that they must keep his covenant, and be to him a kingdom of priests and a holy nation (Exodus 19:3–6). These terms of the covenant are spelled out in the Ten Commandments. You shall have no other gods before me; honor your father and mother; you shall not commit murder or adultery—these commandments spell out what was already contained in the Lord's activity, that he is a *just* God who hates injustice and oppression. His people must become as he is.

THE FALL

But how had mankind been reduced to its sorry condition, from which it could be rescued only by divine intervention? The answer is: *sin.*

Those parts of the Old Testament that precede the account of the exodus were not the first to be written. They are imbued with a knowledge of God and of sin which Israel had learned through divine revelation from the time of the Exodus on, during the following centuries of reflection and experience. The first chapters of Genesis relate how God had made man in his own image, and how man "remade" himself by sin. It was sin that made it necessary for the Lord to begin a new plan of salvation, a plan which was to be extended to all mankind through the agency of his elect people.

The story of the fall of man in the third chapter of Genesis is a profoundly penetrating story. Man, who originally lived in communion with God, is expelled from the garden because of his disobedience. Sin consists fundamentally in the self-exaltation of man; man wished to make himself the equal of God and to have divine knowledge at his command (knowledge of good and evil). Sin is not only an exterior act of disobedience, but also a manifestation of man's ambition for independence, of his desire to shake off the child-father relation with God, and to set himself up as a rival. "You will be like God," was the tempter's beguilement.

As a punishment for their sin man and woman are forbidden access to the tree of life. Man was not created immortal, but was granted the possibility of eternal life. The tree of life and the tree of knowledge stood in the midst of the garden. Man could eat of every tree; "but of the tree of knowledge you shall not eat" (cf. Gen. 2:9, 17). Man was not satisfied to live as God's child, but wanted to face God as an equal, and this original sin brought death on him. The wages of sin is death.

Chapters 4–11 of Genesis sketch the other consequences in broad outline. Sin reveals itself as a power that places man in a state of servitude from which only a divine intervention can deliver him.

IMAGE OF GOD

Other Old Testament terms for sin bring out other aspects of its nature. It is to miss or to abandon (*chattat*) the straight road. Sin makes man guilty (*rasha*). But fundamentally sin is rebellion (*pesha*). God made man in his image—to be his image and representative on earth, to reflect the very nature of God. Every man stands in relationship to the Lord. Man is God's partner, God has made it possible for man to respond to him. Sin is to refuse to choose God, and, consequently, sin is to break this relationship. God made a covenant with man; sin is a violation of that covenant.

The author of these Old Testament chapters was not directly concerned with the ultimate origins of sin but with its undeniable *existence* in the world. He affirms the fact of the universal diffusion of sin without being concerned to know whether the sins of men are connected with the original sin. The story of the fall explains the self-evident fact that all men are sinners. That there is a relation of cause and effect between the sin of Adam and the sin of other men is a truth which is brought out only by later development in divine revelation.

Yet, by showing that once man has admitted sin into his life, it spreads rapidly and is transmitted from one generation to the next, the author came very close to our present view of original sin.

STONE AGE SURVIVALS

From the beginning of her existence as the elect people, Israel had a true, basic understanding of the nature of moral, religious sin; and this understanding of sin was clarified and deepened by the teaching of the prophets. Nevertheless, we do find attitudes toward sin reflected in the Old Testament that strike us as strange today. These are attitudes which the Israelites already had *before* they became the people of God, attitudes shared with other peoples of their time and which were only gradually transformed under the light of their newly revealed faith. The Old Testament reflects notions about sin which are not yet spiritual in all respects.

People of their time emphasized the idea of separation in thinking about their gods. Their gods were separate, withdrawn, other; that is, "holy." Unless certain specific conditions were fulfilled, contact with the gods or what belonged to the gods ("holy things") was dangerous. Holiness and

consequently sin too, were looked up not as interior qualities, but as something quite material and outside of oneself—
almost like material substances. Holiness was a mysterious
something which could be transmitted almost like a material
substance; sin could be washed away like dirt. In the same
line, what was "holy" (*qodesh*) to one god was "forbidden"
(*cherem*) to another god, and must be utterly, completely,
and ruthlessly destroyed. For some time at least the Israelites
continued to practice such "sacrificial bans." The prophet
Samuel urged King Saul to attack the Amalekites who had
opposed Israel on its way out of Egypt. *"Utterly destroy all
that they have; do not spare them, but slaughter both man
and woman, infant and suckling, ox and sheep, camel and
ass"* (*1 Sam. 15:3*).

DYNAMISTIC CONCEPTION

This ancient conception of holiness as something almost
material is reflected in various passages of the Old Testament.
The most obvious example is the story of Uzzah, the son of
Abinadab. When David was transporting the ark of the covenant from the house of Abinadab to Jerusalem, Uzzah was
driving the new cart on which the ark was being carried.
"And when they came to the threshing floor of Nacon, Uzzah
put out his hand to the ark of God and took hold of it, for the
oxen stumbled. And the anger of the LORD blazed against
Uzzah; and God smote him there because he put forth his
hand to the ark; and he died there beside the ark of God" (2
Sam. 6:6–7).

The idea of Yahweh's holiness is emphasized to such a
degree as to eclipse his other moral perfection. A story such
as this expresses the point of view of the priestly class eager

to uphold their priestly privileges. The inspired writer makes use of a traditional way of thinking to make his point.

Sin was connected not only with guilt, but also with defilement and uncleanness. Contact with certain persons or things, or even an unwitting violation of a divine law could bring an uncleanness which had to be removed by some rite of expiation. The Old Testament contains many such prescriptions and rites (Lev. 4:1–6:7).

But this is not the last word of the Old Testament on sin. As with all other things that Israel borrows from her environment, her notions of sin had to be brought into conformity with her revealed faith, or eventually cast off. The conception of material, unconscious sin clashes in a sense with the character of the Lord as revealed in his activity—a just, moral God, who regards only a deliberate disobedience to his will as sin.

UNCLEANNESS

Ritual prescriptions still persisted throughout the whole Old Testament period however. Such prescriptions are especially numerous in the latest texts of the Pentateuch, although many of them are of a more ancient origin. Many of the specific sins which are mentioned there are ritual offenses, such as contact with dead things or various forms of uncleanness, or the breach of food *tabus*.

At times when Israel had to shake off remnants of her pagan past, or fight off new dangers of relapse into paganism, these prescriptions must have had their purpose and could rightly be regarded as the law of God. Furthermore, those who gave so large a place to the expiation of ritual and technical offenses seem to have been motivated by this thought:

if even these were to be treated with such seriousness, with what horror the more grievous moral sins would be regarded. Men should hold the will of God in such awe that they will be filled with concern over the most trifling of prescriptions.

Nomadic peoples tend to have a strong sense of communal solidarity and responsibility. Israel retained a good deal of this sense long after she had settled down in Canaan, an expression of this is found in her thinking about sin. Sin not only brings guilt upon the sinner but also affects the community as a whole.

The Bible does not think of man as an isolated individual but in his relationships to other men in the community. The Bible expresses this by the idea of covenant. The covenant of Sinai bound the Israelites to the Lord and to one another as a people. Sin is precisely that which damages the community or the covenant, that which threatens solidarity. God, who grants life and order, has fixed the laws which safeguard normal life. The life of the whole people is closely linked to God, who sustains that life. Every sin weakens the life of the community.

JESUS SAVIOR

An understanding of both the individual and communal aspects of sin is necessary to the understanding of the mission of Christ. His mission was to free mankind from sin and its effects—the New Testament makes this emphatically clear. Indeed, the name Jesus means, "The Lord saves."

An angel assures the perplexed Joseph that Mary had conceived of the Holy Spirit: "She will bear a son, and you will call his name Jesus, for he will save his people from their sins" (Mt. 1:26). John the Baptist appeared in the wilderness, "preaching a baptism of repentance for the forgiveness of sins" (Mark 1:21). He hails Jesus as "the Lamb of God, who takes away the sins of the world" (John 1:29). Jesus' own proclamation of the Gospel involved repentance: "The time is fulfilled, and the kingdom of God is at hand; repent and believe in the gospel" (Mark 1:14). In his parables, especially, Jesus makes it clear that he came to help sinners. At the last supper Jesus explains that his death, and the sacramental commemoration of his death, is for the forgiveness of sin: "Drink of it, all of you. For this is my blood, the blood of the covenant, shed for many for the forgiveness of sins" (Mt. 26:28). And the risen Jesus established his church and commissioned his apostles to carry on his work, "that repentance and forgiveness of sins should be preached in his name to all nations" (Luke 24:47).

In the time of Christ many Jews made ritual prescriptions an end in themselves and observed them with a care they did not bring to the observance of the more ethical and spiritual requirements of the Law. It was this frame of mind that led to Christ's scathing denunciation of the Pharisees. "Blind guides, straining out a gnat and swallowing a camel. . . . You clean the outside of the cup and dish, but inside they are full of robbery and self-indulgence!" (Mt. 23:24–25). Thus Jesus brings the idea of moral sin to the fore again.

ATONEMENT

But Jesus did not come into the world merely to change men's *thinking* about sin. His mission was to come to grips with sin in the most realistic sense, to overcome, to undo its work, and thereby to restore mankind to fellowship with God (at-one-ment). This he did by freely offering himself as a sacrifice on behalf of all sinners.

The blood of the Passover lamb sprinkled on lintel and doorpost stayed the hand of the destroying angel (Ex. 12:21–23) and the yearly renewal of the Passover sacrifice was a commemoration of Israel's redemption from Egyptian slavery by the Lord's hand. II Isaiah speaks of a Suffering Servant of Yahweh who would willingly accept suffering and death to bring salvation to the ends of the earth. Like a lamb he is led to the slaughter; he is wounded for our transgressions, making himself a guilt offering (*asham*) (Is. 53:7, 5, 10).

Jesus made it known that his death would achieve what the death of the Servant was expected to achieve. His passion and death took place at the time of the Passover, and at the last supper he linked his death with the New Covenant: "This cup is the New Covenant in *my* blood, which is poured out for you" (Luke 22:20).

Under the Old Covenant on one day of the year, the Day of Atonement, the high priest took the blood of the sin-offering through the Temple Veil into the Holy of Holies and sprinkled the mercy-seat (*kapporeth,* "propitiatory"). Thereby the high priest led the Divine Presence back into the Holy of Holies from which it had been driven by sin. The justice of God, writes St. Paul to the Romans (3:24) has been manifested through faith in Jesus Christ, "the ransom (*kofer*) provided in Christ Jesus, whom God put forward as a mercy-seat (*kopporeth*) by his blood, to be received by faith."

FLESH AND BODY

St. Paul offers an even more penetrating explanation of how Jesus overcame sin. Through his incarnation, death, and

66

resurrection, Jesus replaced a solidarity of sin by a solidarity of redemption and salvation.

All men are *flesh* (the Greek word *sarx*). For St. Paul this does not mean any part of man, his sensuality, for example, as it does for us today. For St. Paul flesh means the whole man, man in the solidarity of earthly existence. Flesh is not evil in itself. God created man flesh and at the same time created him in his own image. As a result of sin, however, man as flesh has been separated from God. Because of sin man has also lost his original gift of immortality; death has entered the world. In St. Paul's vocabulary flesh "stands for man in the solidarity of creation in his distance from God."[1]

But St. Paul also refers to man as *body* (the Greek word *soma*). Man as body gives the same picture as man as flesh— man in his solidarity with all other men under power of sin. Yet there is a difference: flesh stands for man, in the solidarity of creation, *in his distance from God;* body stands for man, in the solidarity of creation, *as made for God.*

The body will see resurrection and inherit the kingdom of God, but the flesh will not.

WORD BECOME FLESH

Jesus, the Son of God, overcame sin by becoming flesh, and then breaking the power of sin over flesh. In becoming flesh Jesus identified himself with the body of flesh in its fallen state, insofar as that was possible for him, without himself becoming a sinner. He took "the nature of a slave" (Phil. 2:7), passing under the dominion of death. The Father sent Jesus "in the likeness of sinful flesh" (Rom.

1. J. A. T. Robinson, *The Body,* Chicago: Allenson, 1952, p. 21.

8:3); "he made him to be sin who knew no sin" (2 Cor. 5:21).

But sin and death were not able to gain mastery over Jesus in the flesh. The forces of evil could not turn him into a sinner. All they could do was kill him. But this act was in reality an admission of their defeat. It was only through the flesh that evil had any power of temptation, but Jesus put flesh aside when he died. For Jesus was really the master throughout—he *freely* put off the flesh. This is what the sinner cannot do, because the flesh has power over him. That Jesus had freely put aside the flesh was shown clearly by the resurrection of his body. Death could have no hold on him, since sin had found no foothold in him.

The last link in this chain of salvation is our baptism. The victory over sin which Jesus won on the cross is realized in us through baptism. Through baptism we have repeated the process of the cross in our flesh. Our old self has been crucified with Jesus, "in order that the body of sin may be destroyed" (Rom. 6:6). Just as Christ died "unto sin" (Rom. 6:10) rather than through sin, so in baptism we also die "unto sin" (Rom. 6:2).

BODY OF CHRIST

Redemption is not something that Jesus won *for us,* it is not entirely vicarious. Redemption is something that Jesus does *in us.* Again and again St. Paul speaks of our doing something "with Christ," and specifically, "suffering-together-with-Christ, being crucified, dying, being buried, and rising-together-with Christ from the dead."

Through baptism we have died to sin and the flesh with

and through the crucified body of the Lord. We are now in and of his body which is the Church. United to Jesus in the sacraments we are so truly a part of his body that all that happened in and through that body in the flesh is repeated in us now.

Since Christ is our head and we are his members, his life is not something outside us, but is communicated to us and flows into us. Instead of one person living and dying, satisfying and meriting for another, it is rather as if one person was living and dying, meriting and satisfying for himself. "Christ, as Head, delivered us His members from our sins; just as a man by a meritorious work done by his hands, might redeem himself from a sin he had committed with his feet" (S.T., III, 41, 1).

6.

SALVATION

"Salvation" in the Old Testament comes from a Hebrew word (*yasha*) which originally seems to have implied the idea of space and breadth: to be in a spacious environment or to be at one's ease. A more current, derived sense centers upon the idea of *deliverance:* deliverance from illness, danger, war, bondage, or death. Accordingly "salvation" could mean to be cured, to be successful, to be victorious, to be freed. As we look at it today, this deliverance (salvation) could imply something originally quite natural. As God's plan of salvation was progressively revealed, salvation was seen to entail man's deepest and most far-reaching needs.

In his wisdom God chose to impart salvation to mankind through one people, Israel, the chosen people. God *delivered* Israel from Egyptian bondage ("The LORD *saved* Israel that day from the hand of the Egyptians," Ex. 14:30) and entered into a covenant with the Israelites at Sinai. This was, practically speaking, the starting point of Israel's existence as the people of God. It shaped their concept of salvation, as it did most of their other religious ideas.

As an act of deliverance, the Exodus displays the qualities that characterize salvation in the older section of the Old Testament. It is communal, concerned with the good of the people as a whole rather than that of the individual. In its immediate effects, at least, it was limited, concerned only with the chosen people, and it represented a temporal benefit, deliverance from bondage.

BEGINNING OF HOPE

This first great deliverance, however, was a revelation of the Lord's character, his justice and mercy. By the same token, Israel's duties were also revealed since God's people had to be like him. It also gave Israel hope for the future. The covenant is the foundation stone of the salvation hope. This first act of salvation would be followed by others, even greater ones, if Israel was faithful to the covenant.

Through this and later experience the Lord stood forth as the savior par excellence. The Lord is the "Rock of Israel's salvation" (Deut. 32:15); when the Israelites forsook God they "forgot God, their savior" (Psalms 106[105]:21). Israel's victories are saving acts of the Lord. Several of the best known proper names of the Bible are formed from the word "salvation" (*yasha*). Hosea means "salvation"; Isaiah and Joshua, "The Lord is salvation." "Jesus" is a variation of Joshua.

How fitting that "Hosanna" should be connected with the book of Psalms, the prayer of the chosen people. It means "Save now!"

INSTRUMENTS OF SALVATION

Salvation is from the Lord but at times he chooses to work through others. Victories won by men are in reality the work of the Lord. After the invasion of Palestine, the Lord worked especially through "judges," warrior champions to whom he imparted a special measure of his saving power. The Lord commanded Gideon: "Go in this strength of yours and save Israel from the hand of Midian; do not I send you?" (Judges 6:14). Confronted by his enemies, Gideon sought a sign from God "if he will save Israel by my hand" (6:36).

Later a like measure of the Lord's saving power was granted to the kings of Israel. When King Saul delivered Jabesh-gilead from the hand of the Ammonites, he declared: "Today the Lord has brought about deliverance in Israel" (1 Sam. 11:13).

In these instances, the true source of salvation is further indicated by a reminder (Judges 6:9; 10:18) that it was Yahweh who brought Israel up out of Egypt and that their present need for deliverance is due to their betrayal of the covenant.

The special role in the Lord's salvation passes from Saul to David and his house. Speaking to Saul of David's victories over the Philistines in an attempt at reconciliation, Jonathan tells his father that through David, "the Lord brought about a great deliverance for all Israel" (1 Sam. 19:5). The Lord's "anointed," the messiah (*mashiach, Christus*), the "Son of David," will be his special instrument in the realization of his plan of salvation (messianism).

ESCHATOLOGY

In these instances, as elsewhere in the Old Testament, in general, salvation appears as a collective and national deliverance rather than an act of liberation of an individual. Also it is hardly possible to speak of salvation in the abstract but only of salvation of the elect people in particular situations, in the face of particular threats to their well-being. In

73

the Old Testament Israel's messianic hope was always colored, so to speak, with national and political shades. It was assumed that salvation would be marked by the re-establishment of the throne of David in Jerusalem.

But even this limited expectation did turn Israel's thoughts to the future—to a time of judgment and fulfillment, to an end time to be followed by a new age (eschatology). This hope also opened up the perspective of future broadening and deepening of the concept of salvation.

The prophet Micah, a younger contemporary of Isaiah, stresses his individual share in salvation. The Lord will spare him when he punishes Judah. "As for me, I look to the Lord; I hope in the God who will save me; my God will hear me" (7:7). Jeremiah declares that the Lord will impart salvation by re-establishing the house of David:

> *Behold, days are coming, is the oracle of the Lord,*
> *when I will raise up for David a righteous Branch,*
> *and he shall reign as a true king and be wise,*
> *executing justice and righteousness in the land.*
> *In his days Judah will be saved*
> *and Israel will dwell securely.*
>
> *Jeremiah 23:5–6*

Salvation will be found in a "kingdom of God," the messianic kingdom.

KINGDOM OF THE LORD

The Old Testament expectation of salvation reached its high point in the postexilic prophet, II Isaiah. Lest the original pattern of salvation be forgotten, the return from Babylon is represented as a second exodus (41:17–20). But the return from captivity and the restoration of the elect people in Palestine is only a prelude to the establishment of the kingdom of Yahweh.

> *How beautiful upon the mountains,*
> *are the feet of him who brings glad tidings,*
> *who announces peace, who brings good news,*
> *who announces salvation,*
> *who says to Sion:*
> *"Your God rules."*
>
> *Isaiah 52:7*

"Bringing glad tidings, good news," became, by way of the Greek translation of the Old Testament, the origin of our word "Gospel." The Gospel is "the Good News of Salvation."

The kingdom of Yahweh will be both universal (51:5) and eternal (45:17). The salvation granted in this kingdom is so extraordinary that it is likened to a new creation. "The hand of the Lord has done this; the Holy One of Israel has created it" (Is. 41:20). When the Lord grants this salvation, death itself will be annihilated: "He will destroy death forever, and the Lord God will wipe away tears from all faces" (Is. 25:8).

In a number of the psalms, we see the Lord granting deliverance from sickness and other misfortunes which are looked upon as punishments for sin. Since salvation in these cases presupposes the forgiveness of sins, this individual salvation takes on a more spiritual aspect. That the psalmists were conscious of the moral basis of salvation is also shown by their conviction that only the humble and contrite of heart can call the Lord their savior.

APOCALYPSE

In the later centuries before Christ, many came to despair of salvation in the present order, which they considered so evil that it could only come under condemnation. They looked forward to a salvation beyond the present order, an "apocalyptic" salvation. The end time will be ushered in by a time of universal upheaval and destruction, followed by the judgment of God for which the dead will be raised up. Then the Messiah will appear and establish the eternal Kingdom with new heavens and a new earth (Daniel 12).

The bits of Old Testament revelation can be arranged into a mosaic from which the form of the true Savior emerges dimly. Naturally it is easier for us who have known Jesus to fit the pieces in place than it was for those who were awaiting his coming. Very few had all the pieces at hand. Many had fashioned an idea of the Savior in the light of their ambitions. Some of these must have been so blinded that they could not use what they had at hand. Some refused to accept what they clearly saw.

TIME OF SALVATION

Jesus could not allow himself to be taken for the kind of savior most of his contemporaries had fashioned for themselves. At the very time he was revealing himself to men as the awaited savior he had to correct men's notions of the savior.

Let men know that the time of fulfillment has arrived—this was the first step in Jesus' self-revelation. It was begun already by his Precursor. "Repent, for the kingdom of heaven is at hand," John the Baptist proclaimed. "Even now the axe is laid at the root of the trees" (Mt. 3:2, 10). And when Jesus began his own public life, he began his self-revelation by going about doing things that the Scriptures had said the promised savior would do, especially working miracles and teaching the poor.

Jesus' miracles are a sign that the kingdom has come, and there could be no kingdom without the messiah. John the Baptist sent two of his disciples to ask Jesus if he was "he who is to come." Jesus answered merely that they should go and report to John what they had seen, that "the blind see, the lame walk, the lepers are cleansed, the deaf hear, the dead rise, and the poor have Good News preached to them" (Mt. 11:5).

On a number of occasions after working a miracle of healing, Jesus said: "Your faith has saved you." This is the type of salvation to which we have become accustomed in the Old Testament and the words could equally be translated: "Your faith has healed you." But it is also made clear that the salvation that Jesus grants can be more than physical healing. After the sinful woman bathed and anointed his feet, Jesus said to her: "Your sins are forgiven you . . . your faith has saved you; go in peace" (Luke 7:49–50).

SAVED BY BLOOD

The scope and depth of the salvation Jesus came to bring emerges most clearly perhaps from his identifying himself with the Suffering Servant of II Isaiah. The Suffering Servant brings salvation to the ends of the earth by freely offering himself as a vicarious sacrifice—sacrifice on behalf of others.

> *He was pierced for our offenses,*
> *he was crushed for our sins;*
> *for our peace the chastisement was on him,*
> *and with his stripes we are healed.*
>
> *Isaiah 53:5*

The Servant offers his sacrifice precisely to win for others deliverance from sin.

The Servant's sacrifice is likened to that of the Passover lamb and the guilt offering of the Old Law. "Like a lamb that is led to the slaughter . . . he makes himself a guilt offering (*asham*)" (Is. 53:70, 10).

Jesus, who manifested himself to the world as the promised Messiah, also believed that his death would achieve what the death of the Servant was expected to achieve. His passion and death took place at the time of the Passover, and, at the last supper, Jesus linked his death with the New Covenant when he declared: "This cup is the New Covenant in my blood, which is poured out for you" (Luke 22:20).

At the time of the Exodus, the Israelites were delivered from bondage and death by the blood of the Passover lamb sprinkled on their doorposts. For the Israelites, from the time of the Exodus on, the sacrifice of the Passover lamb was a sacred memorial of the Lord's act of deliverance. The sacrifice of the Lamb of God is the Lord's definitive act of deliverance and redemption for all men.

The angel tells Joseph that he should name the child Jesus ("The Lord saves"), "for he shall save his people from their sins" (Mt. 1:21). When the infant is presented in the Temple, Simeon rejoices:

Now, Master, you can, according to your word,
let your servant depart in peace;
for my eyes have seen your salvation,
which you have prepared before the face of all the peoples,
Light *to illumine the Gentiles,*
Glory *of your people Israel.*

Luke 2:29–31

These texts express the firm conviction of the primitive Church regarding the salvation won and granted by Jesus.

NEW MOSES

For Jews of Old Testament times the deliverance out of Egypt stood forth ever more clearly as the Lord's great act of election. And since in this act of deliverance the Lord had given powerful evidence of his intention to save Israel, the sacred story of the Exodus came to be looked upon as a guarantee that God is perpetually active in delivering his people. Thus it came about that the Jews shaped their anticipation of salvation through the Messiah according to the pattern of the historical Exodus under Moses. The Messiah would occupy the key position in the definitive deliverance as Moses did in the first. The Messiah was expected to repeat what Moses had done. This expectation had a firm basis in the words to Moses: "I will raise up for them a prophet like you from among their brethren" (Deut. 18:18).

St. Matthew's gospel, especially, underlines Jesus' role as the New Moses. The similarity between the birth and childhood of Moses and Jesus is emphasized. The book is divided into five parts in imitation of the Pentateuch; the Sermon on

79

the Mount is the New Law given by the New Moses; the ten plagues of Egypt are replaced by ten miracles, ten acts of salvation (cc. 8–9).

A Hebrew of the Hebrews (Phil. 3:5), St. Paul makes full use of the Old Testament preparation. He makes some forty references or allusions to the Exodus in his epistles. For the Jews the Passover celebration was a memorial of the Exodus deliverance. But it was much more. This feast of commemoration was understood to imply that those who took part in it became one with the Exodus generation itself. Jews of today look on it in the same way. Almost every page of the Hagadah, the ritual for the Passover ceremony (*Seder*) gives expression to the thought: "Every man in every generation must look upon himself as if he personally had come forth out of Egypt. It was not our fathers alone that the Holy One redeemed, but ourselves also did He redeem with them." Similarly, it is not "they" but *we* who are said to have wandered for forty years and to have been fed upon manna in the wilderness.

As a Jew, then, it was altogether natural for St. Paul to consider the Exodus story as written about his own generation. But as a Christian, he knew that he belonged to the definitive exodus under Jesus, the Messiah.

BAPTIZED INTO JESUS

The idea of baptism, of being washed free of sin and its effects, marks all stages of God's plan of salvation in St. Paul's thought. "Our fathers all passed through the sea and were all baptized into Moses" (1 Cor. 10:1–2). When God called Israel out of Egypt to make it the people of his covenant, Israel had to pass through the Red Sea to arrive at Sinai, where the covenant was established. This "baptism into Moses" implied the putting away of their pagan way of life. Arising out of the sea, Israel was a purified people, worthy of adoption into the covenant of God.

When a non-Jew wished to be converted to Judaism, he was baptized. This associated him symbolically and sacramentally with the historical acts through which the election of the chosen people took place. By his baptism the proselyte departed from Egypt, marched through the Red Sea, and was received into the covenant. A saying of the rabbis had it that "when Israel received the law at Sinai, he was like a new-born child, one day old." Another common expression said the same thing of the proselyte.

As a Christian, St. Paul looked upon Jesus Christ as the New Moses, effecting the new exodus of salvation. The starting point of this new exodus, and the counterpart of the actual departure from Egypt, is the death and resurrection of Jesus. "Or do you not know that, when we were baptized into Christ Jesus, it was into his death that we have all been baptized. We were buried therefore with him by baptism into death, in order that, as Christ has risen from the dead through the glory of the Father, so also we might live in a new life" (Rom. 6:3–4).

"As through circumcision and proselyte baptism the Jewish proselyte is incorporated into the people of God and becomes a partaker of God's act of salvation as recorded in the Exodus narrative, and primarily in the crossing of the Red Sea, so the *Christian* proselyte, receiving Christian baptism, becomes a partaker of Christ's act of salvation, His death and resurrection. As the Jewish proselyte becomes by baptism *one* with the Exodus generation, so the Christian through baptism becomes *one* with Christ in His death and resurrection."[1]

The elect of the first Exodus were fed heavenly manna and drank the water from the rock: "our fathers . . . were all baptized into Moses in the cloud and in the sea, and all ate the same spiritual food and all drank the same spiritual drink" (1 Cor. 10:2–4). On the level of fulfillment, the Eucharist is the viaticum of the pilgrims of the New Exodus.

JESUS SAVIOR

An Old Testament attribute of *God,* the title "Savior," was conferred upon Jesus on the basis of faith in him as the Risen Lord. The Jews had reserved the title "Lord" (*kyrios* in its Greek form) to God. But from the time that Jesus' divinity blazed forth in his resurrection, ascension, and the coming of the Spirit, Christians had a watchword: "Jesus is *Kyrios!*" St. Peter ends his Pentecost discourse by declaring: "Let all the house of Israel therefore know assuredly: God has made him both Lord and Christ, this Jesus whom you, you crucified" (Acts 2:36).

The title of "Savior" (*soter*) supplements the title "*Kyrios,*" with emphasis on Jesus' work of atonement and redemption. Apparently it came into use only after the title "*Kyrios*" was well established. Rare in the older New Testament writings, it appears with increasing frequency in the more recent writings. Then "Savior" could have become a special title of honor only where Greek was spoken. In

1. H. Sahlin, "The New Exodus of Salvation according to St. Paul," in *The Root of the Vine,* New York: Philosophical Library, 1953, p. 91.

Aramaic, " 'Jesus Soter' would have been 'Jeshua Jeshua.' "[2]
In connection with other important titles added to the name
Jesus it eventually became part of the Church's ancient
ichthys creed. The first letters of the Greek phrase: "Jesus
Christ, God's Son, Savior" spell out the Greek word for
"fish" (*ichthys*). In Christian symbolism, therefore, the figure
of a fish evokes faith in Jesus Christ as our divine Savior.

2. O. Cullmann, *Christology of the New Testament,* Philadelphia: Westminster, 1959, p. 245.

7.

KINGDOM OF GOD

The Old Testament has a forward look. Something lies ahead; indeed, the best is yet to be.

This outlook on time and history has so become part of our way of thinking that it is hard for us to conceive of any other. Actually this outlook comes to us only through revelation and its reflection in the Scriptures. Apart from revelation men thought quite differently.

The Old and the New Testament relate God's acts of salvation—the measures he took to impart salvation to alienated mankind. Basically this revelation took the form of saving acts. God did certain things in the past at specific times and places. God acted in time and history. He began a project which is carried out progressively, of which the accomplishment is not the same as the point of departure. Biblical time is linear—an ascending line moving toward a goal, with a yesterday, today, and tomorrow, a true past and an authentic future.

Without revelation men thought of time as a circle, not as a straight, ascending line with a beginning and an end. Time brings nothing new. Things are reproduced in an eternal cycle. In the ancient Near East the "history" of the cosmos was preserved and transmitted by myths. But this "history" could be repeated indefinitely, in the sense that the myths served as models for ceremonies that periodically reactualized the tremendous events that occurred at the beginning of time.

ETERNAL RETURN

An act was acknowledged only if it had been previously posited and lived by a divine being. An action acquired meaning and reality solely to the extent to which it repeated a primordial act. There is no place in this scheme of things for time and history as we understand them.

In Greek thought, history was thought of as a process of degradation, a fall from a state of innocence on a spiritual, timeless plane to one of guilt on a material plane, which alone has time. According to this point of view, salvation necessarily implied the annihilation of time. This had to be done either by ritual myth, which periodically regenerated the cosmos and society by contact with primordial acts of gods and heroes, or by mysticism—freeing oneself from time to be united with the divinity.

For the Greeks, eternity meant a complete absence of time. The Bible, on the other hand, uses one word (*aion*) for both time and eternity. Time, from creation to the end, has definite limits, but is open at both ends. Eternity is unlimited time.

God acts because he saves. When God acts, a project is carried out progressively. The Bible has a forward look and Israel has hope for the future. Mankind enjoyed a period of innocence and bliss at the opening of history, but the climax and crown of history lies in the future. And since Yahweh is the Lord of time and history, the climax will come when his will shall be fully carried out.

The Lord rules time and history at all times. But some of his creatures to whom he has given the gift of free will have disobeyed him and oppose his will. But when the Lord's will is fully realized then he will rule completely. This "day," the

"Day of the Lord," will be the day of the full establishment of God's Rule, the *Kingdom of God*.

STARTING POINT IN COVENANT

United with Yahweh in the covenant communion, Israel first experienced the Lord as God of the Covenant and Savior, proving his fidelity time and again. This relationship is the source of the hope of salvation and the profound consciousness of mercy and fidelity that marks the faith in God of the Israelites. This being the historical starting point of their conception of God, the chosen people naturally related the idea of God's rule and providence first and foremost to themselves and the country in which they lived, and only in the second place to the world of the nations and to nature in general. From belief in the Lord as Savior, the faith of Israel moved outward to the idea of the Lord as ruler of all the nations, and then to that of the Lord of creation.

The Lord's rule over all nations is first made *explicit* in Amos, the first of the "writing prophets." Yahweh's greatness as creator came to be of central importance only in II Isaiah.

Yet, the Lord's rule over all the nations seems to be implicit in his delivering his people from Egypt. "The Sinai covenant . . . in fact created a domain with an overlord and subjects; henceforward the idea of the *Kingdom of God* is in the air."[1] If the Lord's power over the Egyptians was so great, could his power over other nations be less? The doctrine of Yahweh's rule over all peoples remained latent for a time. The gods of the other nations may have continued to

1. W. Eichrodt, *Theology of the Old Testament,* Vol. 1, Philadelphia: Westminster Press, 1961, p. 40.

exist, in some sense at least, in the conscious mind of the Israelite. Yet the deliverance from Egypt implies that the Kingdom of God is absolute and universal. Yahweh is the true, living God, the God of gods. His very greatness causes other gods to melt away.

The Lord rules history and guides it towards its final goal: his Kingdom on earth. Hope of salvation would be groundless without this reality.

DISRUPTION AND MAINTENANCE OF NATURE

For some two hundred years after the making of the covenant, the Israelites, unlike all other peoples of the time, had no king to rule over them. The Lord was their king and they were his people. Israel was the Lord's Kingdom. And when we consider the way kings were looked upon at the time, and the history of the Davidic kingdom, this kingless period appears providential.

During the Exodus and at Sinai, the Lord had manifested his might in a way that corresponded to his people's needs at the time. By the miracle of the Exodus and the phenomena that accompanied the making of the covenant at Sinai (thunder, lightning, trembling of the earth), the Lord demonstrated that he could disrupt the established order. When the Hebrews were made the Chosen People they were nomads and their well-being was to be achieved by disrupting the established order and dispossessing the owners of the land (Canaan) that had been promised them. If they were faithful to the covenant, the Lord's power would be directed against their enemies.

The change from desert life to a settled existence in Palestine presented a serious challenge to Israel's belief in God's rule. Once they had settled on the land and begun to till it, the idea of Yahweh they had gained in the desert would no longer suffice. At this point the Israelites were changing from nomads to farmers. Their well-being would henceforth depend not on the disruption of the established order, but precisely on its maintenance. If Yahweh were nothing but a destroyer God, he would have to be abandoned for the Canaanite religion, which, it was believed, could insure the fertility of the land. The Israelites would also have to have a king to rule over them, since the king's role in religious worship was all-important.

KING IN RITUAL MYTH

The king was a religious as well as a political figure. His function was to maintain harmonious relations between human society and the divine powers, which were more or less identified with the powers of nature. The idea of nature and natural laws not having arisen, the cycle of seasons was thought of as a strife between divine and demonic powers, powers of order and chaos.[2] From season to season human society moved in harmony with nature through a recurring sequence of religious festivals. To say that the people celebrated these festivals would be inadequate. Ritual acts were not merely symbolic, but powerful to achieve the results desired. No one could foresee the outcome of the struggle between the deities. The celebration of the festivals could

2. Cf. J. McKenzie, S.J., *The Two-Edged Sword*, Milwaukee: Bruce, 1956, pp. 51 f.

insure the triumph of the god of order and fertility and thus insure fertility for flock and field for the coming year.

The king's part in this cultic ritual was all important. In Babylon, for example, the king re-enacted the part of the divine king of the gods. His death was bewailed in the scorching heat of summer. In the autumn, during the great New Year's festival, the finding and liberation of the god was re-enacted. So too was the battle that the divine king had fought and won for creation against chaos at the dawn of history. The king's resumption of power and sacred marriage were thought to determine the destiny of society for the coming year.

If the Chosen People had had a king when they first came into Canaan, the temptation to look upon him in the same way as their pagan neighbors looked upon their kings would doubtless have been too strong for them. Even as it was the temptation to turn to the worship of Baal was an extremely strong one and many times it seemed that Israel's faith was to be submerged in Canaanite culture.

FAITH AND CULTURE

The ritual myth was reassuring and sensuously gratifying. To forego it for the pure and demanding worship of the Lord demanded a real act of faith and renunciation. Many Israelites thought that they could worship both Yahweh, the Lord of the Heavens, and Baal, who controlled the fertility of the soil. "How long will you go limping with two different opinions?" the prophet Elijah challenges the Israelites during the time of King Ahab and his wicked queen, Jezebel. "If the Lord is God, follow him, but if Baal, then follow him" (1 Kings 18:21).

This contest between Israel's faith and Canaanite culture was to rage for centuries. And the people's failings in this regard could not but call down the Lord's judgment upon them. This judgment was the disasters they suffered, including the downfall of the kingdom.

In the events of the Exodus and the conquest of Canaan, the Lord demonstrated that he was no mere natural power, immanent in nature. He was above nature and could disrupt the established order and turn it to his own purposes. The Israelites learned this aspect of the Lord's rule well. But was Yahweh also the upholder of the natural order, the preserver of the regular rhythm of the seasons, by which the fruitfulness of the land is renewed year by year? Here lay Israel's temptation.

KINGDOM OF ISRAEL

That they were a people without a king for two hundred years after the conquest of Canaan may well have kept Israel from succumbing entirely to the temptation. With no king to rule over them, they were organized into a twelve-fold tribal confederacy. To meet a particular danger, the Lord would raise up a military champion (a judge), by the gift of his spirit. A human king must never be for Israel what he was for the pagans—a necessary bond between the people and the divine power. This would be a sin against their faith in Yahweh and their belief in his Rule (Kingdom).

Yet, when the Philistines with their iron weapons and chariots seemed on the point of destroying them, the Israelites became convinced that the loosely-knit confederacy could not save them. They began to demand a king "like the nations, to fight our battles" (1 Sam. 8:19). Both a favorable and an unfavorable attitude toward the adoption of kingship is reflected in the Old Testament. Considering the pagan attitude toward kingship, it is not surprising that there were those who interpreted it as a rejection of Yahweh himself.

This unfavorable attitude is reflected in 1 Samuel 8, for example. The elders of Israel come to Samuel, saying: "You are old and your sons do not walk in your ways; now appoint us a king to govern us like all the nations" (v. 5). Samuel prays to the Lord for enlightenment and the Lord replies that he should grant their request, but goes on to add: "They have rejected me from being king over them" (v. 7).

With reluctance and misgivings on the part of many, Israel became a kingdom. But it was essential that kingship be introduced in such a way as not to compromise Israel's belief in the Lord's own Rule. The solution was an understanding of the king's *messiahship*. The king is not a divine being by nature. But he has received a consecration (an "anointing") at the hands of Yahweh's representative (the prophet), in a holy spot, with a special gift of the Lord's spirit. In this way he is made the Lord's special instrument in the work of salvation.

LORD OF NATIONS

Just as the change from a nomadic to an agricultural life led to a fuller understanding of the Lord's rule, so also did the change from a tribal confederacy to a monarchy. The Israelite now becomes a subject and citizen in a state, and his state becomes involved in international relations. The idea of Yahweh's lordship and kingdom must be projected onto a new plane. Yahweh is transcendental lord in the sphere of international politics as well.

The prophets drove the lesson home and their words were confirmed by events. Yahweh presides over and manipulates the nations as he presides over and manipulates the forces of nature. Yahweh can both uphold and destroy here too. He can both defend Israel against her enemies and use those enemies to scourge her.

Yahweh's power over the nations is shown by the destruction of many kingdoms by Assyria and then the destruction of the Assyrian empire itself. The fall of the Northern Kingdom proved to Judah that Yahweh would punish unfaithfulness. The prophets, from Amos on, said that the Lord would not spare even his Chosen People. When, therefore, the nation fell in 586 B.C., it was clear that Yahweh himself had punished his people's disobedience. Assyria was only the rod of his anger. The Assyrian king called himself the "great king" and "king of kings" but he is only the Lord's instrument. Yahweh is king and king of kings.

Yet the frequent triumph of evildoers and the misery of the just often made this fundamental conviction difficult to sustain. The Lord's sovereignty is not manifested in this world where a number of earthly kingdoms exercise their sway. But the Lord must one day assert his sovereignty, and man longed for the coming of that "day," the "day of the Lord"—a day which the prophets declared would surely come.

ESCHATOLOGY AND APOCALYPSE

It is almost to be expected, then, that during and after the exile, there is increased emphasis on the "Lord's kingship," especially its future and universal character. The suffering of this epoch only strengthened the desire for the coming of the Lord's ultimate and definitive (eschatological) rule.

Thus the Lord says through Ezekiel: "As I live, I swear it—it is I who will be king over you, with a mighty hand and outstretched arm, and with wrath poured out. . . . I will make you pass under the rod" (20:33, 37). And in a much more compassionate tone, II Isaiah announces the Rule of God as glad tidings, the good news of definitive salvation: "How beautiful upon the mountains are the feet of him who brings good tidings . . . who says to Sion: 'Your God rules' " (52:7). From this time on the theme, "the Lord rules," comes with increasing frequency in the Scriptures, especially in the psalms (e.g., 96–99).

The "day" would come when the Lord would take up his reign over all the earth, either directly, or through his agent, a new ideal David (messianism). Some persons, despairing of salvation within history, looked forward to the end of this world-age. At that time, amid spectacular manifestations of divine power, God would establish his reign (*apocalypse*).

We note that in these passages it is a question of "the Lord ruling" rather than "the kingdom of God." But late Judaism is marked by a strong tendency to avoid attributing actions directly to God and to use abstract notions instead. Thus the "God dwells" of the Old Testament becomes the *shekina,* God dwelling among his people; "God speaks" becomes the Word of God; "God rules" becomes the Kingdom of God. Yet the Kingdom of God continues to denote primarily the fact that God is king rather than the place or extent of his Kingdom. His kingship, reign and sovereignty are stressed. The alternative "Kingdom of Heaven," means the same thing, since "heaven" in this sense was merely a conventional Jewish usage whereby the taking upon one's lips of the name of God might be avoided.

Jesus drew on all this thought and language to describe his work in the world. He affirms that the Kingdom of God transcends all earthly kingdoms and distinguishes between its inauguration here on earth and its final consummation. The germ of this doctrine is found already in the prophet Daniel. Jesus presents the message of the Kingdom as "good news"; glad tidings of peace, pardon, abolition of sin and death, and divine friendship restored—a way of speaking that has its source in II Isaiah and the kingship psalms.

When Jesus said at the beginning of his preaching: "The time is fulfilled, the Kingdom of God is at hand," he was proclaiming an *event,* the sovereign decision of God now to manifest and exercise effectively his supreme sovereignty. God is now setting about the task of putting straight the evil plight into which the world had fallen. The Kingdom of God is a personal, gratuitous intervention of God, who through his Son, manifests his sovereignty, changing the course of history, carrying out his will regarding mankind and destroying the empire of Satan.

Jesus' power over the demons attests that a decisive assault was being made upon the spiritual powers of evil. "If it is by the Spirit of God that I drive out devils then the Kingdom of God has come upon you" (Mt. 12:28). The Kingdom of God means primarily the rule of God, but it also includes a realm or kingdom. The same action that establishes the Reign also establishes a Kingdom where God is fully recognized as

King. The Kingdom in its present, earthly phase, is the Church.

God who rules eternally by right, has ruled in a special way since the establishment of the Kingdom through Jesus. In that sense, the Kingdom has already arrived. But in another sense the Kingdom is still to be established, for Jesus taught us to pray, "Thy Kingdom come." While Jesus ushered in the definitive Kingdom, its consummation will come only on the "last day" when Jesus will come again in power to judge.

8.

MESSIAH

When God acts to save, a project is carried out progressively. This gives the Bible its forward look and Israel her hope for the future. The Bible looks forward to the climax of history—to the "Day of the Lord," when the Lord's will to save will be fully realized.

This Biblical hope for the future gave rise to several rather elusive technical terms. A Greek word (*eschatos*) meaning "last" was used to form the term "eschatology"—"having to do with the last things." "Messianic" is almost a synonym for "eschatological." "Messianic" is the adjective form of a Hebrew word (*mashiach*) meaning "anointed one," which translated into Greek became *christos; christus* in Latin. All the Scripture passages referring to the Day of the Lord or the Golden Age are commonly referred to as *messianic*.

While several categories of persons are spoken of as "anointed ones" in the Old Testament, the term *mashiach* designates in particular the *king of Israel*. Anyone to whom God assigned a special mission for his people could bear the title. There are indications that priests were actually anointed with oil, at least in postexilic times (Ex. 29; Lev. 8; Zech. 5:14). But this application of the term to prophets, patriarchs, and the people itself, seems to be based on metaphor. In Is. 45:1, Cyrus, a foreign heathen king, bears the title because God assigns him a special task in the execution of the divine plan of salvation.

ANOINTED SAVIOR

"Messiah" (*mashiach*, "anointed one") designated in particular the king of Israel. In 1 Samuel we read that the Lord revealed to the prophet Samuel: "About this time tomorrow I will send to you a man from the land of Benjamin, and you shall anoint him to be prince over my people Israel. He shall save my people" (9:16). The man sent was Saul the son of Kish. Saul came and ate with Samuel and stayed the night. "Then Samuel took a vial of oil and poured it on his head, and kissed him and said, 'Has not the Lord anointed you to be prince over his people Israel?'" (10:1). Later Samuel was to anoint David in a similar way (1 Sam. 16:13).

By this unction the king became "the anointed one of Yahweh." The anointing symbolized the consecration of the king's person to the Lord, a consecration that was often visibly sealed by the Spirit of the Lord's taking possession of the "messiah." The descent of the Spirit of the Lord accompanies the anointing of both Saul and David. "Samuel took the horn of oil, and anointed David in the midst of his brothers; and the Spirit of the LORD came mightily upon David, from that day forward" (1 Sam. 16:13).

LORD'S INSTRUMENT

The reception of the Spirit certainly implies a transformation. "God gave him another heart" it is said of Saul (1 Sam. 10:9). It indicates a change from the status of a private person to that of a charismatic ruler, a consecrated representative of the Lord. The anointing was carried out by the Lord's representative, the prophet, and in a holy place. Kingship in Israel is "by the grace of God." Other titles that the "messiah" bears indicate the divine origin of his office. He is the "son of God." "I will be his father and he shall be my son" (2 Sam. 7:14). The Lord is the true king of Israel and the king-messiah exercises this divine function in his place. It was only on these terms that the People of God could accept a king at all.

The Davidic dynasty came to occupy an exceptional place in the ideas of the Chosen People. The decisive factor in this development was Nathan's prophecy to David. David had resolved to build a temple to house the ark of the covenant, but the Lord sent the prophet Nathan to tell David that it was not for him to build the temple. The Lord will build David a a house, a dynasty, that will last forever. *"The LORD will make you great; the LORD will make you a house. When your days are finished and you lie down with your fathers, I will raise up your son after you, who shall come forth from your body, and I will establish his kingdom. It is he that shall build a house for my name, and I will establish the throne of his kingdom forever. . . . Your house and your kingdom shall be made sure forever before me; your throne shall be established forever"* (2 Sam. 7:11–13, 16).

David's glorious reign led the Israelites most naturally to picture the realization of the divine promises under the image of a powerful and victorious king, who will establish his dominion over all the enemies of his people, over all the earth. David's family was closely associated with the religious centers of the people as well. David captured Jerusalem and Solomon built the Temple to house the ark of the covenant.

KINGDOM FOREVER

Because of Nathan's prophecy and its promises of perpetuity it was natural that "the anointed one of Yahweh", the "messiah," should gradually become an "eschatological" figure.

We know from the Scriptures that before the time of fulfillment came, the Lord acted in a special way on a number of occasions to sustain and direct messianic hopes. When it seemed that the Davidic line would be extinguished, God sent the prophet Isaiah to inform King Ahaz that his line would continue. "The Lord himself will give you a sign. Behold the *almah* shall conceive and bear a son, and shall call his name Emmanuel" (Is. 7:14).

Several passages in the same prophet sing of a Davidic leader figuring as the divine representative in universal government. A shoot from the stump of Jesse, he will rule with the equity characteristic of the Golden Age to come. "With justice he shall judge the poor, and decide with equity for the meek of the earth" (11:4). The consequences of his rule will be universal, "the earth shall be full of the knowledge of the Lord, as the waters cover the sea" (11:9). The prophet Micah, a contemporary of Isaiah, sings of a ruler to come forth from Bethlehem Ephrathah, "whose origin is from of old," but whose rule shall extend to all the earth and shall be exercised in the name of God and in his power (5:2, 4).

Even when the remaining portion of the nation was falling to the Babylonians, the prophet Jeremiah was proclaiming the continuance of the line. "Behold, the days are coming, is the oracle of the Lord, when I will raise up for David a righteous Branch, and he shall reign as true king and be wise, executing justice and righteousness in the land" (23:5).

And sometime later the prophet Zechariah also refers to Jerubabel, the governor of the postexilic community, as The Branch (6:12). Despite the worst disasters, the conviction perdured that the Anointed One of the house of David was to play the key role in the realization of Israel's hope for the future. But nowhere in the Old Testament, it would seem, is the term "messiah" (*maschiach*) itself used clearly and exclusively of the "One who is to Come," the ultimate Messiah.

MESSIAH OF END-TIME

"Messiah" gradually became an eschatological figure, but this does not mean that in the opinion of all he would appear in an other-worldly setting. Many Jews took it for granted that an earthly kingship would be necessary in order to introduce future salvation. The hope of the eschatological appearance of a king of Davidic descent became particularly active as Jewish nationalism developed under the rule of Greece.

The Jews thought of the ascending line of time and history as divided into three stages by two crucial events. There was the time before creation, the time from creation to the Day of the Lord, and the time of the final age that followed. Later, probably through contact with Persian dualism, a bipartite division was superimposed on the earlier tripartite division. Time was divided into "the present age" (*aion*) and "the age to come." This change coincided with a change prophecy to apocalypse. This "present age" was despaired of and would have to be destroyed or utterly transformed before the final age could be brought in.

At first, it seems, it was thought that the Lord himself would bring in the final age. Then there were those who assigned this task to the Messiah. In late Jewish apocalypses we find a combination of these two ideas. The messianic king will bring in a provisional kingdom and the Lord himself will bring in the final kingdom. This idea of an *interim kingdom* occupies an important place in the Christian understanding of the messianic kingdom.

The classical expression of the prevailing messianic expectation of New Testament times is found in the Psalms of Solomon, a first century B.C. writing that was never accepted as inspired. The author of this text prays to the Lord to raise up the Messiah, son of David, that he may purge Jerusalem from pagans, break sinners with a rod of iron, and destroy the godless with the word of his mouth. After this judgment he will gather together a holy people and establish a kingdom devoid of injustice, wherein everyone will be holy. The Messiah himself, called the "Anointed (*Christos*) of the Lord," is free of sin; wise and just by the gift of the holy spirit. He does not place his confidence in horses or arms; he does not gather silver or gold to wage war; he trusts only in the Lord.

Did Jesus present himself to his contemporaries as the awaited Messiah? The answer to that seems to be: yes and no.

KING OF THE JEWS

During the trial of Jesus, the high priest Caiphas asked him: "Are you the Messiah, the Son of the Blessed?" (Mark 14:61). Caiphas intended this to be a trap. The title had strong political overtones in the popular estimation and if Jesus said "yes," Caiphas could turn him over to the Romans as a political rebel. If Jesus said "no," he would be discredited in the eyes of the people. Jesus' answer seems to have been, in effect, "You say so, not I." And he added immediately: *"But* I tell you, hereafter you will see the *Son of Man* seated at the right hand of Power, and coming on the clouds of heaven" (Mark 26:64).

Translating the title "Messiah" into Roman terminology, Pilate asked Jesus: "Are you the King of the Jews?" Again Jesus answered, "You say so, not I." Jesus neither refused nor accepted the title unequivocally. At Caesarea Philippi, Jesus asked his disciples, "Who do men say that I am?" Peter answered: "You are the Messiah." In reply, Jesus "gave them strict orders not to tell anyone about him. And he began to teach them that the Son of Man must suffer many things, and be rejected by the elders and the chief priests and the scribes, and be killed, and after three days rise again" (Mark 8:30–31). When Peter rebukes Jesus for such an idea, Jesus gives a frightening command: "Get behind me, Satan."

When Satan came to tempt Jesus in the desert after his baptism, the climax and the meaning of the scene is indicated by the third temptation, when Satan "took him to a very high mountain, and showed him all the kingdoms of the world and their splendor; and he said to him, 'All these I will give you, if you will fall down and worship me.' Then Jesus said to him, 'Begone, Satan!' " (Mt. 4:8–10). Satan's offer to give Jesus mastery over all the kingdoms of the world corresponded to the common Jewish hope for their expected Messiah.

CORRECTED MESSIANISM

There are many indications that in this matter too, St. Peter represented the thinking of the other apostles. The ambition of the sons of Zebedee (Mark 10:35) and the apostles' desertion of their master during the hour of his apparent defeat show what thoughts were in their heads.

Jesus saw the hand of Satan at work in the contemporary Jewish conception of the Messiah. He did not proclaim himself the Messiah and he forbade others to do so (Mark 1:24, 34 f.; 2:11 f.; 5:43), knowing that such a proclamation would lead to a false conception of his mission. When the question of his messiahship arose, he chose to speak of the Son of Man or the Suffering Servant of the Lord.

Yet it is also clear that Jesus did not directly reject the title and office of Messiah but only the Jewish understanding of the title. From the beginning Jesus was fully conscious of his special mission with regard to the Old Covenant. "Do not think that I have come to do away with the Law or the Prophets. I have not come to do away with them but to fulfill" (Mt. 5:17). Jesus came to fulfill completely the divine Lawgiver's original intention. It is for this reason that he could say that the Law would perdure "till heaven and earth pass away" (Mt. 5:18).

This is to say that from the beginning Jesus was fully conscious that he was the perfect realization of the messianic promises of the Old Testament. St. Luke's gospel gives expression to this conviction, recording the words of the boy Jesus after he had remained behind in the temple: "Did you not know that I must be about my Father's business?" (2:49).

While avoiding and rejecting explicit messianic titles with their explosive connotations, Jesus nonetheless defined his mission. He assumed other meaningful titles, especially that of Son of Man, and he preached the Kingdom of God as a present reality. Above all, he revealed himself and his mission by the things that he did.

ONE WHO IS TO COME

When John the Baptist sent two of his disciples to ask, "Are you the one who is to come, or are we to expect some other?" Jesus answered with a catalogue of his works (Mt. 11:4–6). While he refused to dazzle the crowds with spectacular miracles, he held them responsible for their failure to believe after what they had seen and heard, "The men of Nineveh will arise at the judgment with this generation and condemn it; for they repented at the preaching of Jonah; and what is here is greater than Jonah" (Mt. 12:41).

Some grasped the meaning of Jesus' words and actions, and once at least, on the eve of his death, Jesus allowed himself to be hailed by a clearly messianic title. As he rode into Jerusalem on Palm Sunday, those who went ahead and the others who came behind shouted:

Hosanna!
Blessed is he who comes in the name of the Lord!
Blessed is the kingdom of our Father David that comes!
Hosanna in the highest!

Mark 11:10

The nature of Jesus' messiahship, then, was none too easily imparted or grasped, but in all the gospels the primitive church's conviction comes home to us. Jesus is the Messiah sent by God. On the whole the infancy narratives wish to show that Jesus is the Messiah announced by the prophets. Matthew's genealogy centers around the Christ Child's Davidic descent and Matthew underlines Jesus' birth in Bethlehem, the town of David.

Repeatedly the evangelists show God confirming Jesus'

messianic dignity. John the Baptist carries out the role of the forerunner. And at the time of Jesus' baptism, John the Baptist saw the Spirit of God descending like a dove and a voice from the heavens said, "This is my beloved Son, with whom I am well pleased" (Mt. 3:17). This is in fulfillment of the sayings of Isaiah, who foresaw that one day a shoot should come forth from the stump of Jesse, upon whom the Spirit of the Lord should rest (Is. 11:12), and of whom it should be said:

> *Behold my servant, whom I uphold,*
> *my chosen, in whom I delight;*
> *I have put my spirit upon him,*
> *he will bring forth justice to the nations.*
>
> *Isaiah 42:1*

9.

THE LAMB OF GOD

Skeptics used to think that they had scored a point against the uniqueness and supernaturality of the religion of the Old Testament every time they could point out that the Israelites shared a certain religious idea with their pagan neighbors or celebrated a religious feast whose origins could be traced back to pagan times and practices. But there are not many who are so naive today.

For one thing, the gestures and material means at man's disposal to express his interior sentiments and experiences are limited. And man's reaction when confronted with the divine or what he considers to be divine is always more or less the same. Therefore it is not at all surprising that different religions have certain exterior traits and certain rites in common, even when there is no historical contact between them.

It is even less surprising then that Hebrew worship should share certain beliefs and rites with pagan Semitic peoples to whom they were related and with whom they had lived. The Hebrews were not chosen to be God's people because they were better qualified than others. In religious matters they thought as other people of their time did, and the covenant did not transform them over night.

MEANING FOR ISRAEL

When the people of God broke their way into Canaan, Joshua called a great convocation for the renewal of the covenant made at Sinai. He reminds the people that beyond the River Euphrates, in Mesopotamia, their fathers had served "the gods." And it is evident that Joshua is already fearful lest the Israelites turn to the "gods of the Amorites (Canaanites)" in whose land they now dwelt (Joshua 24: 14 f.).

How ancient a certain rite may be, or what significance it may have had at first, have little bearing on our reading of the Bible. A rite practiced by the Israelites may be quite similar to a pagan rite. A certain festival may have originated in pagan times. Be that as it may, the all-important thing is the meaning of this rite or festival as observed by the people of God. The meaning attached to rites and festivals depends upon the idea that people had of the divinity. Rites and festivals had to mean something different to the Israelites, because Yahweh is different from the gods. And as the Israelites got to know Yahweh's nature more fully, they had to gradually purge their worship of him of all those elements that are not in conformity with his nature.

When men believe that the correct performance of a certain rite will constrain the god they are worshipping to grant the favors sought, they are practicing magic. There may be rites that were of a magical nature in their primitive form and remained so among pagan Semitic peoples, but they could not remain magical among the People of God.

SACRIFICE

Among the ancient Semitic peoples, worship already expressed itself in ritual prayer, and, above all, in animal sacrifice. The pagan Semites did not think of their gods as standing wholly outside nature. In some sense the gods were part of the natural universe and not entirely exempt from the general limitations of physical existence. The gods were felt to be akin to man in inner structure, and consequently they responded to prayers and gifts just as human beings would. The god was felt to be in need of food, drink, clothes and servants and *sacrifice* was one part of the total service rendered to the god.

The most common and probably most primitive sacrifice was one in which the blood of the victim was poured on the altar or on the ground and the fat and other parts were burned on the altar for the deity. The meat provided a feast for the sacrificer, his family, and his friends.

In our sophistication we may think that the ancient Semites had reduced everything too much to the human level. But in its own imperfect way their sacrifice expressed a number of timeless religious truths—man's utter dependence on the deity for life and the things that sustain life, his belief in a community of exchange between himself and the deity, and communion with the deity in a sacrificial meal of holy food.

The Hebrews therefore were no strangers to sacrifice when Yahweh made them his people. Since they were a pastoral people, sheep were valuable domestic animals and the lamb was one of the most important sacrificial animals.

PASCHAL LAMB

Their principal festivals occured on the occasions on which shepherds were rewarded for their labors (birth of the lambs in the spring and sheepshearing) and these festivals included the sacrifice of lambs.

The Hebrews then, when they became God's people, were probably not strangers to a spring festival during which lambs were sacrificed. But it doesn't at all follow that the Israelite Passover was the result of a purely natural development of this ancient sacrifice. How ancient a certain rite may be or what significance it may have had at first or in pre-Mosaic times, have little bearing on our reading of the Old Testament. The all-important thing is: what did the Passover sacrifice mean to the People of God?

For the Israelites the slaying and eating of the Passover lamb was not only a true sacrifice but a sacred memorial, the commemoration of a supernatural fact—the Lord's intervention in history to save them. The slaying of the Passover lamb was inextricably associated with the Exodus. The Israelites were bidden to celebrate it in order to remember their deliverance from Egypt and what that deliverance had meant to them as a people.

The blood of the slain lamb sprinkled on lintel and doorpost stayed the destroyer's entry (Exodus 12:21–23), and the yearly renewal of the sacrifice was to be a continual reminder. "When your children ask you, 'What does this rite mean for you?' you shall reply, 'It is the sacrifice of the Passover in honor of the Lord, who passed over the houses of the people of Israel in Egypt, when he slew the Egyptians but spared our houses' " (Ex. 12:26–27).

The sacrifice of the Passover lamb reminded the Israelites of all God's mighty acts for their fathers, including their redemption from Egyptian slavery and the divine election of Israel in grace. It was meant to serve as the vehicle for a yearly renewal of the Covenant and of their loyalty to God.

When Jesus, the one to whom all events of the Old Testament are directed, appeared in the world, he was addressed as the "Lamb of God" by John the Baptist. And St. Paul says of him that our redemption comes through faith in him, "whom God put forward as the means of propitiation by his blood" (Rom. 3:25).

LAMB-IMAGERY

But before the time of realization came, 1200 years were to pass from the time of the sacrifice of the first Passover lamb. And during all those centuries, not only was the lamb important in the economic life of the Chosen People, but it also occupied the central position in their most significant religious observance, the Passover, and was used besides in many other sacrifices. Under those circumstances, it was inevitable that the lamb's peculiar qualities, striking in themselves, should make a deep impression on the people. The Israelites, like other Semites, were particularly gifted in the use of comparisons, parables, and the like, and there were few things in the world that lent themselves so readily to this purpose as the lamb.

Because of its gentle, affectionate nature, the lamb appears in Nathan's parable against King David as the appropriate image for the devoted daughter (2 Sam. 12:2–3). The wolf-lamb contrast is such a natural one, there is no telling how ancient it may be. When the book of Isaiah wishes to describe the blessedness of the age of realization, the age of the Prince of Peace, it does so in exaltedly poetic terms:

> *Then the wolf shall dwell with the lamb,*
> *and the leopard shall lie down with the kid;*
> *and the calf and young lion shall graze together,*
> *and a little child shall lead them.*
>
> *Isaiah 11:6*

Sacrifices, both the Passover and others offered at other times during the year, expressed fundamental religious truths for the Israelites from their earliest days. But as time went on, sacrifice, and especially the sacrifice of the lamb, came to have a new meaning for them. While sacrifices expressed basic religious truths from the earliest days, the Israelites do not seem to have felt the need or the inclination to identify themselves with the sacrificial victim. To see in the fate of that victim and the spirit with which it accepts its fate a picture or an examplar of their own was not considered.

SACRIFICIAL VICTIM

But as Israel's national disasters increased and especially as many innocent persons saw themselves involved in disaster that they had in no way caused, they began to see that the life and death of the sacrificial lamb somehow pictured their own.

When the people of Anathoth secretly plotted against Jeremiah, the prophet says that he "was like a gentle lamb led to the slaughter" (11:18). Jeremiah identifies himself with the lamb only in his defenselessness, not yet possessing the ability to discern a value in the sacrifice itself, and to identify himself with the lamb also in its humble, uncomplaining submission.

The prophet Ezekiel likens the whole nation of Israelites to a flock, helpless and defenseless under the hand of wicked shepherds who lead them astray and subject them to all kinds of depredations. "So they were scattered, for lack of a shepherd, to become food for all the wild beasts; they were scattered. My flock wandered over all the mountains and high hills; my sheep were scattered over all the face of the earth, with none to look after them or to search for them" (Ez. 34:5–8).

SUFFERING SERVANT

But in II Isaiah a significant new development appears. II Isaiah is the anonymous author of that portion (cc. 40–55), of our present book of Isaiah that is addressed to the Israelite exiles in Babylonia. Several times there appears in the poems of these chapters a mysterious figure designated as "the servant of Yahweh." The Servant is described in at least four different passages (42:1–4; 49:1–6; 50:4–9; 52:13–53:12). These are called Servant Songs. The Servant is to be Yahweh's agent in the work of salvation.

But the really new and significant thing is the way in which the Servant brings salvation to the end of the earth. The Servant is a suffering servant; he wins victory through suffering.

The first three poems tell us of the Servant's mission and the gentleness and persistence with which it is undertaken. His mission is to Israel and then to the whole world and it will involve him in great suffering. It is only when we come to the fourth song (52:13–53:12) that we learn that the Servant's mission will involve him in death and that his suffering and death are not merely a consequence of his mission but its very organs.

Speaking for their people, the rulers of the nations expressed astonishment that such an unlovely, despised figure could be the chosen agent of God. Formerly they had thought that he was being stricken and smitten by God for his sins.

> *We others, we esteemed him stricken,*
> *smitten by God, and afflicted. . . .*
> *Like a lamb that is led to the slaughter,*
> *as a sheep before its shearers is dumb,*
> *so he opened not his mouth.*
>
> Isaiah 53:4b, 7b–c

Now they understand that all along the Servant has been suffering in their stead—taking upon himself the consequence of their transgressions that they might again have "peace."

> *For our peace the chastisement was on him*
> *and with his stripes we are healed.*
>
> Isaiah 53:5

In the last verses of the poems, the Servant's redemptive work stands forth so clearly as sacrificial in character that he is likened to the Passover lamb. "Like a lamb that is led to the slaughter, so he opened not his mouth." The Servant's sacrificial death is not a fate that men or circumstances have imposed upon him. It was part of Yahweh's redemptive purpose, in which the Servant freely acquiesces.

> *Yet it was the will of the LORD to bruise him;*
> *he has put him to grief;*
> *when he makes himself a guilt offering (asham).*
>
> 53:10

In the worship of the Second Temple, the trespass or guilt offering (*asham*) was made to atone for theft of human or divine property. The Servant is freely offering himself as a vicarious sacrifice—sacrifice on behalf of others.

NEW COVENANT IN BLOOD

This is the high point of the Old Testament. It is the strongest link uniting the Old Testament with the New, and, at the same time, some remarkably clear evidence that Jesus' life and work were part of a divinely arranged economy of salvation. For Jesus who manifested himself to the world as the promised Messiah also believed that his death would achieve what the death of the Servant was expected to achieve. And not only was Jesus' death determined and carried through by his enemies, but Jesus repeatedly and emphatically foretold what was to happen. And then his passion and death took place at the time of the Passover, and at the last supper, Jesus linked his death with the New Covenant when he declared: "This cup is the New Covenant in my blood, which is poured out for you" (Luke 22:20).

At the time of the Exodus, the Israelites were delivered from bondage and death by the blood of the Passover lamb sprinkled on their doorpost. Whatever significance the sacrifice of the lamb may have had before, from the time of the Exodus, the sacrifice of the Passover lamb was for the Israelites a sacred memorial of the Lord's act of deliverance. At the last supper, Jesus, the Lamb of God and the Suffering Servant, charges the ancient festival a second time with new significance. The sacrifice of the Lamb of God is the Lord's definitive act of deliverance and redemption, for all men.

As Jesus himself had indicated during his public life, all

aspects of the Old Testament lamb-imagery received their actualization and full realization in himself. He was both the new passover lamb, the Lamb of God, and the embodiment of the lamb of II Isaiah which is mentioned in a context wholly concerned with the vicarious sacrifice of the Servant of the Lord. Jesus is truly "the Lamb of God who takes away the *sins* of the world" (John 1:29, 36).

Writing to the Christian converts of Asia Minor, St. Peter reminds them that they had been "redeemed . . . by the precious blood, as it were of a lamb without mark or blemish —the blood of Christ" (1 Peter 1:18–19). And in his first epistle to the Corinthians, St. Paul affirms: "Christ, our paschal lamb, has been sacrificed" (5:7). This allusion is all the more valuable because it is incidental to an exhortation. The Jews regarded the putting away of old leaven at Passover time as symbolic of moral cleansing. So now let Christians shun all evil, "for Christ our paschal lamb has been sacrificed."

Reflecting the teaching of Jesus himself, the evangelists bear witness to the same fulfillment in more subtle ways, as, for example, in their accounts of the baptism of Jesus. In their eyes the baptism represents the anointing of Jesus with the Holy Spirit to the office and work of the messianic Servant of the Lord. As in times past the king was anointed and became the Anointed of the Lord, and in a later time the priests were anointed, so now Jesus, the Suffering Messiah, is anointed with the Spirit of the Lord.

The divine significance of Jesus' baptism is expressed by the "voice from heaven" which identifies Jesus with the Servant of the Lord of II Isaiah. "You are my Son, my Beloved; you are my Chosen" (Mark 1:11). The reference is to the first of the Servant Songs: "Behold my servant, whom I uphold; my chosen, in whom I delight; I have put my spirit upon him" (Is. 42:1). Jesus, the Lamb of God, *qui tollit peccata mundi,* who bears and takes away the sins of the world, bears the sins of the world to the baptism of repentance as later he was to bear them to the baptism of his death.

As the "spirit of God moved over the face of the waters" (Gen. 1:2) at the first creation, so the Spirit hovers over the waters of the Jordan, as Jesus is consecrated as the "Lord's Anointed," the first born of many brothers who through their own baptism into his death in the Holy Spirit shall be made corporately into the New Creation.

10.

THE SON OF MAN

Jesus came into the world to "fulfill" the hopes of Israel, the covenanted people of God. The Chosen People's history had followed a pattern of infidelity, punishment, and survival of a small remnant. They had been made a kingdom and had lost their kingdom because of their infidelity. In the course of this experience all their hopes became concentrated in the coming of an Anointed One, a Messiah, who would appear to execute the Lord's judgment on all the world. This judgment was to include judgment on their enemies (their power would be broken) and establishment of the Kingdom of God. And the Jews for the most part identified the Kingdom of God with the Kingdom they had once enjoyed.

It is easy to be wise after the fact, but we can see today that Jesus "fulfilled" or "accomplished" these hopes only after he had elevated, spiritualized, and sublimated them, as his heavenly Father had decreed. Jesus had to reveal himself as the Messiah and establish the Kingdom of God. At the same time he had to correct the notions of his contemporaries as to what the Messiah and the Kingdom of God should be. He was the promised Messiah but not a military hero. He established the Kingdom of God but it was not a political kingdom. And above all he came to be a mediator of divine life, which is possible only for the Son of God.

How could the Jews be made to accept these ideas? It is

certain that they would surprise, disappoint, and even scandalize the majority of Jesus' contemporaries.

MESSIANISM RESHAPED

The full secret could be revealed only after a long preparation. Until that preparation was complete, Jesus chose to refer to himself by a mysterious title, the "Son of Man," which said neither too much nor too little about him. It was a title that could mean different things to different people, but whose true and full meaning the disciples of Jesus were invited to gradually discover for themselves. We meet the title many times in the Gospels, but only on the lips of Jesus and as applied to himself, and only before his resurrection. Some Jews could possibly recognize that his use of this title was an affirmation that he was the Messiah, but these would be few in number. To start with Jesus chose to reveal himself simply by doing the things that it had been said that the Messiah would do, especially by working a multitude of miracles. He called himself the "Son of Man," a title whose true meaning men of good will would discover if they cooperated with the graces Jesus held out to them.

Jesus, for example, in his preaching to the people, might have proclaimed himself as the "Son of David," and nearly every Jew would have recognized his use of this title as an affirmation that he was the Messiah. The establishment of the kingdom of David had been providential and Yahweh had identified himself with David's dynasty forever. The Lord had promised David through his prophet Nathan that he would "establish the throne of his kingdom forever" (2 Sam. 7:12).

THE BRANCH

And when the dynasty of David seemed faced with extinction, the prophet Isaiah spoke most glowingly of the Prince of Peace to come.

> *A shoot shall come forth*
> *from the stump of Jesse,*
> *and a branch shall grow out of his roots*
> *And the Spirit of the LORD shall rest upon him.*
> *Isaiah 11:1–2*

Even the prophets of the postexilic period, Haggai and Zechariah, express the conviction that the Kingdom will be restored under the co-leadership of the high priest and the Jewish governor, Zerubbabel, a descendant of Jehoiachin, the last king of Judah. Speaking through the prophet Zechariah, Yahweh says that: "Behold, I will bring in my servant, the Branch" (Zech. 3:8). The sign of Zerubbabel's messianic authority is that he will complete the building of the Temple. "Thus says the LORD of hosts, 'Behold a man, whose name is the Branch: where he is something shall grow (and he shall build the temple of the LORD)' " (Zech. 6:12). For Zechariah the word "branch" is the term for the messianic king, the descendant of David's line. It was only later that the word "messiah" ("anointed one") took on the special meaning of *the* Anointed One, the Messiah.

The Gospels bear abundant witness to Jesus' Davidic descent. Of the Son she was to bear the angel Gabriel said to Mary: "The LORD God will give to him the throne of his father David" (Luke 1:32), and the child was born in the town of David, "which is called Bethlehem" (Luke 2:4).

When Jesus began to work his miracles, "All the crowds were amazed and said, 'Can this be the Son of David?' " (Mt. 12:23).

MESSIANIC SECRET

During the early part of his public life, however, Jesus did a most unusual thing. No sooner did he convince persons that he was the Messiah, and no sooner did they begin to proclaim him as the "Son of David," than "he gave his disciples strict orders not to tell anyone that he was the Messiah" (Mt. 16:20). He did this for the same reason he referred to himself as the "Son of Man" rather than the "Son of David." The latter title was too explosive, politically speaking. For five centuries the Chosen People had been smarting under heathen domination. It took very little to touch off fanatical, suicidal revolts in Jesus' time. These desperate Jews had concentrated nearly all their hopes for national restoration and political revenge on the appearance of the "Son of David." Jesus was the promised "Son of David" but not the kind these people had invented for themselves.

SUFFERING MESSIAH

The term "Son of Man" filled perfectly both the conditions of the time and what Jesus really was, both man and the Son of God by nature. He came as the Messiah but a humble, suffering Messiah. All these ideas are connected in one way or another with the term "Son of Man." The term is used frequently in the Old Testament to indicate a human being pure and simple—just a "man." It occurs most frequently in the prophet Ezekiel (over a hundred times) where the term is used to underline the prophet's weakness and nothingness in the Lord's sight. And he said to me, "Son of man, stand upon your feet, and I will speak with you" (Ezekiel 2:1).

The term occurs once, however, in the Old Testament in a special sense—in the book of Daniel. This book seems to have been composed by an unknown writer during the reign of the Greek ruler Antiochus Epiphanes (175–163 B.C.). This ruler's fanatical attempts to make the Jews adopt Greek paganism led to an armed revolt started by the priest Mattathias, and carried on by his five sons (Maccabean Revolt).

Even before this armed resistance, the inroads of Greek paganism had been combated by the Hasidim (the "loyal or pious ones"), the forerunners of the later Pharisees. Undoubtedly the author of the book of Daniel was one of them. His purpose was to strengthen Israel's faith in the face of persecution. Affirming that the course of history is completely under the the Lord's control, he summoned the Chosen People to courageous faith.

PROPHECY IN NEW FORM

At the time he was writing, it was believed that prophecy had ceased, and it had become a common thing to release writings under the name of some illustrious figure of Jewish tradition. So this writer chose the name Daniel, a traditional pious Israelite according to Ezekiel (14:14), and predates his writing during the Babylonian captivity. So, despite first appearances, the author is looking backward from the present rather than forward into the future, at least when he is tracing out the rise and fall of empires.

But in one sense, the book of Daniel does dwell more on the future than do the writings of the earlier prophets. Daniel belongs to a special class of literature known as *apocalypse* ("revelation").

The entire Bible has a forward look, inasmuch as it looks forward to the climax of history, the "Day of the Lord," the "Kingdom of God," and this is true of the New Testament as well as the Old. Jesus brought in the Kingdom as a present reality and yet its full realization lies in the future. In this sense, it can be said that all Scripture is eschatological, "concerned with last things."

APOCALYPTIC ESCHATOLOGY

However, there is a shift of emphasis as we pass from the eschatology of the prophets to the eschatology of the apocalyptic period.

The prophets of Israel had been concerned primarily about the *present*—about the Lord's judgment on the way the people of God were acting in their time. They touched on the future, and, especially on the end-time and the appearance of the Messiah and the establishment of the Kingdom of God. However, only insofar as these realities might be determined by the present conduct of the people were they discussed.

Apocalypse is prophecy in a new form. Now the interest centers on the end-time, the time of judgment, the "Day of the Lord," which ushers in the New Age, the Kingdom of God. It is asserted with renewed emphasis that this day is close at hand. All this had a particular relevance for people suffering bitter persecution, during a time when history seemed to be controlled by the power of evil. Then too, this type of literature abounds in bizarre visions and strange symbolism which made the writing a "sealed book" (Dan. 12:4) to unbelievers.

BIPARTITE DIVISION

Moreover, in the apocalyptic period the "present age" is despaired of. It is consigned to the power of evil and will have to be destroyed. Then the Lord's promises of salvation will be realized in an entirely new context, in the "age to come." This transformation of thought took place owing to at least two causes: disappointment of high hopes, and contact with pagan way of thinking (Persian and Hellenistic).

A separation is made between the *eternal world of God above* and the *reality on earth below*. The latter is handed over to destruction. And the worlds are separated. In prophetic eschatology, salvation is actualized within the framework of time; there is unity of place and time (this world) and action (it is the Lord who works, if only indirectly through his Messiah). In apocalypse, this unity is broken. The *place* is different: the present world is to be destroyed and the Kingdom of God is to be realized in a "world to come." The *time* is different: the Kingdom of God is to be realized in a timeless eternity. Even the *action* is different: various figures do preparatory work for the coming of the Kingdom (Elijah), while the Messiah becomes the bringer of salvation rather than the Lord directly.

On an older threefold division of time (time before creation, between creation and the Day of the Lord, time of the final age that follows) the apocalyptic age superimposed a bipartite division (present age, age to come). The Kingdom of God as preached by Jesus did not conform perfectly with either expectation. The Kingdom he preached has, as it were, an interim period—the age of the Church. He preached the Kingdom as a present reality but its final consummation lay ahead, as it is still ahead for us. Before the Old Age has entirely passed away the New Age has been brought in, as it were, by anticipation.

All these features play a part in our Lord's use of the title, "Son of Man."

ONE LIKE A SON OF MAN

In the second part of the book of Daniel we find four visions that portray the movement of historical events toward the goal determined by God—judgment on the world and the establishment of the Kingdom of God. Four successive empires are portrayed (Babylonian, Median, Persian, and Greek) each surpassing its predecessor in evil and brutality. In the mind of the writer this increase in evil is a certain sign that history is hastening toward a showdown, and the judgment of God will be pronounced.

In the first vision (chap. 7) we see four beasts rising out of the "great sea." In the popular thought of the Near East, the sea, with its roaring winds and restless waters, was identified with chaos, the power of disorder. To express the transcendence and omnipotence of the Lord, it suffices for the book of Genesis to state that: "the Spirit of God was hovering over the face of the waters" (Gen. 1:2). The four beasts are the four empires and their origin in the sea indicates their hostility to God's order.

The vision of Daniel goes on to explain how the "Ancient of Days" presiding over the Heavenly Council, deprived the first three empires of their dominion and sentenced the fourth, the Hellenistic or Seleucid, to destruction because it had been so monstrously evil. "And behold, with the clouds of heaven," in contrast to the empires' origin from the sea, there comes "one like a son of man," a figure with a human rather than a beastly aspect.

There can be no doubt about what this figure represents in the book of Daniel. Daniel asks for an interpretation and is told that the figure represents "the saints of the most High." "These great beasts, four in number, are four kings, who shall arise out of the earth. But those who shall receive the kingdom are the saints of the Most High, and they shall possess the kingdom forever, forever and ever" (Dan. 7:17–18). Unlike the preceding empires their kingdom shall last forever.

HEAVENLY MESSIAH

Thus the "Son of Man" entered Jewish tradition and entered it to stay. And in the course of time the term was to take on meanings other than that found in Daniel. In later apocalyptic writing not included in the Old Testament a figure appears who is called variously "the Elect One," and "the Son of Man." So now the "Son of Man" is definitely the Messiah. Moreover, it is consistently suggested that there is something that exceeds the human about this "Son of Man." He is closely associated with the Ancient of Days and possesses prerogatives that are almost divine.

In Jesus' time, the expression was used in some Jewish circles to designate a superhuman Messiah. But not all the Jews read the apocalyptic books, and so we find some of them asking: "Who is this Son of Man?"

Here was a term that filled perfectly Jesus' condition and purposes. It was messianic but not political, and it suggested both aspects of his nature, human and divine. When the high priest asked Jesus if he was the Messiah, He answered: "I am; and you will see the *Son of Man sitting at the right hand of Power, and coming with the clouds of heaven*" (Mark 14:62).

Characteristically, Jesus here accepts the title of Messiah and then immediately begins to speak of the Son of Man. In this instance he combines a reference to the Son of Man passage from the prophet Daniel with a reference to Psalm 110(109):1: "Sit at my right hand, till I make your enemies your footstool." "Sitting at the right hand" is inseparably connected with the thought of the priest-king after the order of Melchizedek. Standing before the Jewish high priest and questioned about his messiahship, Jesus speaks of himself as the heavenly Son of Man and heavenly High Priest. His is not an earthly messiahship. This corresponds to the saying preserved in St. John's gospel: "My kingdom is not of this world" (18:36).

There being no ready-made conception of the Son of Man current in the days of our Lord, "Son of Man" meant whatever Jesus taught his disciples that it meant. Jesus made use of it to indicate both his coming sufferings and his future glory and exaltation as triumphant Son of Man.

The Son of Man

The Son of Man "sitting at the right hand of Power, and coming with the clouds of heaven" expresses one aspect of the ideas the expression could suggest, the one that seemed to exceed the human level—the Messiah's ultimate triumph as Redeemer and Judge. But the entirely opposite aspect could also be suggested by the expression—that it was necessary for the Messiah to suffer and die.

"He was instructing his disciples, and telling them, 'The Son of Man will be delivered into the hands of men, and they will kill him; and three days after being killed, he will rise again'" (Mark 9:31). "Behold, we are going up to Jerusalem; and the Son of Man will be delivered to the chief priests and the scribes, and they will condemn him to death, and deliver him to the Gentiles" (Mark 10:33).

The expression on Jesus' lips here evokes the fourth Suffering Servant Poem of II Isaiah. "But he was wounded for our transgressions, he was bruised for our iniquities; for our peace the chastisement was on him, and with his stripes we are healed" (Is. 53:5).

Jesus is the perfect fulfillment of this prophecy also, meriting divine glory for many by his redemptive sacrifice. When Jesus called himself "Son of Man" he was really inviting men of good will to stop and ask themselves: who is he, what is he? That he was a great rabbi was clear, teaching with authority and confirming his teaching with miracles. But he was more, he was a prophet and a great prophet. Many people gave him that title and he did not refuse it.

But if the Precursor is "more than a prophet," (Mt. 11:9), what is he whom John came to announce. Moreover the prophets only asked men to accept their message, while

Jesus asks men to submit themselves entirely to his person. The kind of messiahship he claims for himself is more than human. Jesus made few formal declarations but he offered plenty of evidence in his works.

When Jesus' work was completed and the promised Spirit of truth had descended upon the first Christians, then they "were guided into all the truth" (John 16:13). Then they knew with certainty: the Son of Man is the Son of God. Or as St. Peter declared in concluding his Pentecost sermon: "Let all the house of Israel therefore know assuredly: God has made him both Lord and Christ, this Jesus whom you, you crucified" (Acts 2:36).

11.

The Breath and Spirit of God

The ancient Semites identified their gods in one way or another with the forces of nature, and left to themselves they never came to the knowledge of a being outside and above nature. If the Chosen People did come to a knowledge of a supernatural being, it was not due to their cleverness in religious matters. It resulted from a divine revelation. The eternal, transcendent Lord erupted into their history, made known who he is, something about his nature, and what his plans were for them.

The Lord transcends both history and nature. No force or power in the world is strictly speaking more characteristic of him than any other. The forces of nature were gods to the pagans, but for the Hebrews they were Yahweh's creatures and servants. Yahweh created nature and he can use all its powers to accomplish his purposes in history. In the Exodus Yahweh brings plagues to remind men that "all the earth is mine." He commands the wind to drive back the waters of the Red Sea; his presence is indicated by the thunder and lightning bursting over Sinai. Psalm 104 (103) says it all in a few words:

> *Covered with light as with a garment,*
> *You stretch out the heavens like a tent,*
>   *and lay the beams of your chambers on the waters;*
> *Making the clouds your chariot,*
>   *you ride on the wings of the wind.*   *v. 2–3*

RIDER OF THE WINDS

One can see how natural it is to think of the wind (*ruach* in Hebrew) as an act of God in a special way. Light and intangible, no one knows its limits, and no one can grasp its whence and whither. Of mysterious origin, transcendent and immensely powerful, at times even violent and destructive—power and mystery are the characteristics of the wind, and as they are of the Lord.

Yahweh demonstrated in his great redemptive act, the Exodus, that he is the master of the fiery east wind coming in from the desert. It was by an east wind that he brought the locusts upon the Egyptians (Ex. 10:13). It was by a "strong east wind" that he drove back the waters of the Red Sea for his people to cross. The wind (*ruach*) was the Lord's chief agent in the first great act of redemption and salvation—destroying all that was harmful to his people, strengthening them and sustaining them. The west wind, on the other hand, coming in from the sea, brought rain and fertility for a parched country.

This "wind symbolism" made an indelible impression on the consciousness of the Chosen People. And since *ruach* means "breath" and "spirit' equally well, this usage is the providentially arranged preparation for the revelation of the Spirit of God as sustainer, strengthener, Paraclete.

GIVER OF LIFE

The *ruach* of Yahweh as wind is an apt symbol of power and majesty, and fecundity as well. But if the *ruach* of Yahweh were only wind it could never have become the force that gives *life* to all living things, as it clearly did in the Old Testament.

Interest in Yahweh as the source of life became pronounced during and after Solomon's reign. Up to that time the Israelite's attention had been concentrated on the Lord's great redemptive acts and their consequences. Now for the first time he became deeply conscious of himself as a *person*. Furthermore, the country was more open to outside influences, and most of Israel's pagan neighbors, and especially the Egyptians, shared the idea of the divine breath as life-principle. Israel felt compelled to assert here too that Yahweh alone exercises this function. His *ruach,* now conceived as divine breath, is the life-principle of all creation.

Psalm 104 (103), as we have already seen, celebrates Yahweh as the lord of nature. "He rides on the wings of the wind; he makes the winds his messengers." But later in this same psalm it becomes clear that the ebb and flow of life on earth is dependent upon the breath of the Lord.

> *When you hide your face, they are dismayed;*
> *when you take away their RUACH, they die*
> *and return to their dust.*
> *When you send forth your RUACH, they are created;*
> *and you renew the face of the ground.*
>
> *v. 29–30*

That the Israelites could look upon the wind and the breath of life as manifestations of the *ruach* of Yahweh bears witness to their profound sense of the Lord's power and its presence in the world. It is his function to assure the harmonious operation of the forces of nature, rightly his alone.

SPIRIT MOVES WHERE IT WILL

But these concepts leave no room for divine interventions in the world other than God's normal action on nature and animate creatures. Even in this realm, to be sure, Yahweh is subject to no "determinism," but retains perfect liberty of action. But there is no place in these concepts for God's intervening in history and carrying out intentions quite apart from the normal functioning of the world, and imparting powers to men's souls over and above those necessary for life.

Yet such extraordinary interventions did happen. The Israelites had been the first to experience them. They were acutely aware that they owed their privileged position, indeed, their very existence as a people and a nation to the Lord's extraordinary interventions on their behalf at the time of the Exodus from Egypt and the formation of the Covenant at Sinai. From that time on, such extraordinary interventions were never to cease in their midst. And to what could these extraordinary phenomena be ascribed if not to the *ruach* of the Lord?

As in the case of *ruach* as wind or life-breath, one sees here the same mysterious power to act at a distance, to penetrate to the heart of things, and lift them from their inertia. But now the spirit works on an incomparably higher level.

In the course of time *ruach* as wind progressively took on the aspect of a national phenomenon, while *ruach* as life-breath assumed the aspect of an individualized possession. The "spirit," however, this power that manifests itself in Israel, changed in the opposite direction. It gradually became more interior and spiritual, more clearly distinguished from every purely natural power.

CHARISMATA

The real work of the spirit is interior. The spirit of the Lord works on the spirit of man. Not, however, that the spirit's principal role was to make the recipient "good"—to transform him morally. The spirit was given to enable the recipient to carry out some extraordinary mission assigned to him by the Lord. This is the *ruach* of Yahweh as *charism,* divine activity working in and through the bodily faculties of men.

The two most important "charismatic" offices in Israel were those of judge ("liberator") and prophet.

During the period of the judges the Israelites had no king. When the people of God were oppressed and stood in need of a "liberator," the Lord would raise up a man for the occasion. This charismatic leader carried out his appointed task not by virtue of his own personal qualities and attainments but in virtue of the "spirit of the LORD" that had been given him. Here the charism often appears in its most primitive form: miraculous physical strength that suddenly possesses a man's bodily faculties and uses them to destroy the enemies of Israel.

But with the passage of time, the charism of the spirit became progressively more interior, spiritual, and permanent. Thus it takes the form not merely of physical strength in war but warlike *skill* as well. Then, the spirit imparts skill to fashion the utensils of the tent of meeting and the priestly garments, a development that leads to the concept of charismatic wisdom. In all this the teaching function of the Paraclete is clearly foreshadowed.

When Samuel anointed David king we read that "the

Spirit of the LORD leaped upon David, from that day forward" (1 Sam. 16:13). The expression is awkward and bears
witness to a transition of thought. The *ruach* both takes sudden possession of David as had been the rule in the case of
the judges, and resides permanently, definitively investing the
king with divine power.

PROPHETS

At the same time that the *ruach* was manifesting itself in
the judges, the charismatic liberators, it began to work
through another special class among the Israelites, the
prophets (*nabi*). There too we find the same movement
from exterior, physical manifestations toward more interior
and spiritual manifestations.

The *nabi* appeared as a group or band at first and they
prophesied ecstatically, in a state of dervish-like frenzy, with
song and dance, and incoherent babbling. Their purpose was
to inspire the Israelites to resist their enemies, the enemies of
God's kingdom.

But as time passed the prophets became increasingly aware
that they were more than zealous champions of holy war.
They were bearers of the Lord's *word*. Speaking under Yahweh's spirit it was their primary task to interpret the meaning
of events and to proclaim the will of God in concrete terms.
This they could not do so long as the prophetic band was
acting or singing in unison. So more and more we find individuals standing out from the prophetic band, even breaking with it, to proclaim the Lord's word.

The Breath and Spirit of God

SPIRIT OF CONSOLATION

The theology of the *ruach* reached its greatest development in the Old Testament in II Isaiah. In resting on the Suffering Servant the "spirit of the LORD" works an entirely new effect. Its only function is to transform the Servant's heart and prepare him for his unique mission. His mission is more mysterious and divine than any that have gone before. He is to bring forth "justice" for all peoples.

Divine, too, is the mission of the herald assigned to bring the Good News (Gospel) to Jerusalem: God is coming to deliver them and to build up the ancient ruins.

> *The Spirit of the LORD God is upon me,*
> *because the LORD has anointed me.*
> *He has sent me to bring the good news to the poor,*
> *to bind up the brokenhearted.*
>
> *Isaiah 61:1*

All the essentially *paraclete* functions are gathered together in the herald's activity (preaching of the gospel, the consoling of Israel, the rebuking of her oppressors). So exalted is the herald's prophetic mission that he has need of a special gift of the spirit; no longer of a transitory nature but a permanent endowment. The herald therefore is a type of Jesus, the Prophet par excellence, on whom the spirit rests not for some hours or for some particular message, but whose entire existence is the message of God, the Good News of Salvation, the Gospel.

In the Gospel we read that Jesus, at the beginning of his public life, went into the synagogue at Nazareth and was invited to read and expound the Scripture passage for the day.

137

It was the herald passage from Isaiah. "And rolled up the scroll, gave it back to the attendant, and sat down. The eyes of all in the synagogue were fixed on him. And he began to say to them, 'Today this scripture text has been fulfilled in your hearing' " (Luke 4:20–21). In Isaiah and Jeremiah we also see the spirit descending not only on privileged souls (judges and prophets) but extended to an entire people.

> *Once again there will be poured out upon us*
> *The Spirit from on high;*
> *and the wilderness will become a fruitful field.*
> *Isaiah 32:15*

WATER OF LIFE

Of old the *ruach* brought life-giving rain from the west. So now, as rain that comes to water the parched earth and make it fruitful, the spirit is "poured out" on the entire people. Here the spirit works in a new way. No sudden seizure of a man, no extraordinary behavior, no compelling impulse. The image evokes rather "the fluidity of the liquid which seeps into the most recessed depths and which gradually permeates the hardest substances.[1] The spirit comes as a gift, at the Lord's good pleasure; and, like the rain, it falls on arid ground and impregnates it with life.

Water and spirit have become inseparably united. The Precursor speaks of one who would "baptize with the Holy Spirit." and St. Paul sums up the meaning of it all when he writes to the Corinthians: "It is in a single Spirit that we have

1. J. Guillet, S.J., *Themes of the Bible,* Notre Dame: Fides, 1960, p. 260.

all been baptized, to form a single body—Jews and Greeks, slaves or free men—all were made to drink of one Spirit" (1 Cor. 12:13).

In the Old Testament, therefore, the idea "Spirit" denotes an activity of God's power, God's outgoing activity, which may have a number of effects. It is one of the devices that the Old Testament makes use of to speak of God's action and at the same time avoid too-human modes of expression. Like the ideas "Word of God," and "Wisdom of God," the idea "Spirit" is a reverential way to describe God's initiative and action in the creation and redemption of mankind and the cosmos through Israel.

GIFT OF LAST DAYS

In the latter days of prophecy, a number of prophets (Ezekiel, Isaiah, Zechariah, Jeremiah) stress the activity of the Spirit of God in the New Creation of the last days. The Spirit will rest upon every member of the renewed Israel in a permanent way. The Spirit will impregnate the New Creation with new life. Through the prophet Joel, the Lord declares:

> *I will pour out my Spirit on all flesh;*
> *your sons and your daughters shall prophesy.*
>
> *2:28*

On Pentecost Day St. Peter quotes this passage and proclaims its fulfillment in the events of that day.

Living prophecy in Israel faded out long before the time of fulfillment came. The written Torah came to be thought of as the final and supreme revelation of God and prophecy was held to be in abeyance. A writer who had something to say henceforth adopted a pseudonym—the name of some illustrious personage of the past.

But the doctrine of the Spirit was by no means forgotten: the Spirit was projected into the future. The Spirit's absence at that time underlined the oracles of the great prophets regarding the Spirit's activity during the New Age. The Spirit came to be looked upon as an eschatological element. The conception of the Holy Spirit which is found everywhere in the New Testament is thoroughly eschatological.

SPIRIT OF PENTECOST

With the coming of the Holy Spirit on Pentecost, all that Jesus had said fell into place for the recipients of the Spirit and the Church's faith was fully founded. They understood the nature of Jesus' messiahship and the Kingdom he had preached. They understood fully all that had happened. St. Peter proclaims their conviction. The outpouring of the Holy Spirit fitted in with all else: the eschatological age had arrived. The old order of things had not entirely passed away as the Kingdom was brought in, as so many had expected. The Kingdom is a present reality in an interim period as it were, and looks to its perfect accomplishment yet to come.

The events they had witnessed, the death, the resurrection, and ascension of their Master has brought about this outpouring of the Holy Spirit in accordance with prophecy. Before the death of Jesus the Holy Spirit had been *incognito,* unknown even to the disciples. "For the Spirit was not yet, because Jesus was not yet glorified" (John 7:39). But after

Pentecost the apostles so live by the spirit that the Spirit is seen to form a part of their community, to be one of its members. The Spirit is a *person* who lives with the apostles: "We are witnesses to these things, we and the Holy Spirit, whom God has given to those who obey him" (Acts 5:32).

SPIRIT AND THE KINGDOM

From this vantage point the apostles begin to recall and to understand fully the import of various sayings of Jesus. Jesus had said: "Truly, I say to you, there are some of those standing here who will not taste death before they see the Kingdom of God come in power" (Mark 9:1). In St. Mark's mind, the "Kingdom in power" seems to indicate the Spirit-filled Church he knew.

When the Scribes accused Jesus of casting out demons by the power of Beelzebub, Jesus told the Parable of the House Divided (Mark 3:20–30), and concluded by saying: "Truly, I say to you, everything will be forgiven the sons of men, their sins, their blasphemies, any they may have uttered; but whoever blasphemes against the Holy Spirit will never have forgiveness; he is guilty of an eternal sin" (vv. 28–29).

To reject the Kingdom of God is to reject the very means of salvation, including the forgiveness of sins. Jesus has offered signs of the Kingdom's arrival—the exorcisms which demonstrate the overthrow of Satan's counter-kingdom. The Holy Spirit was at work in these exorcisms and an outpouring of the Spirit was the great sign that the Kingdom had come. To attribute these to Beelzebub is to exclude oneself from the benefits of the Kingdom that Jesus is establishing.

141

"Will never have forgiveness" may well mean: will never have forgiveness in "the New Age of Salvation."

REVELATION OF THE SPIRIT

As the economy of salvation unfolds, therefore, the word "spirit" takes on a stronger and more precise meaning. The personality of the Holy Spirit is not revealed to us from the start. The Holy Spirit first draws our attention to natural phenomena (wind, breath) that reveal his power over the world. Then he reveals himself in the power he imparts to those whom he inspires (judges, prophets, the elect). Finally, his divine personality is revealed through Jesus and the new activity he carries out in the Church after Pentecost.

The various stages of this development reveal the fundamental laws of the Spirit's action, first, in the world, and then in the community of the elect. Since the one God is at work throughout, a basic continuity is evident. Earlier elements are never entirely discarded. Thus even when an entirely spiritual action of the Holy Spirit is described, the wind serves as a term of comparison, to show us the Spirit's mode of action.

The wind animates the fecundating rain; the spirit imparts supernatural efficacy to God's agents and life to all creatures that breathe; the Holy Spirit imparts divine life in the age of the Church. Thus continuity of symbol and the real is maintained.

The age of the Church, the messianic age, is the age of the outpouring of the Spirit. Yet all that God accomplishes now and will accomplish in the future is a replica of what he accomplished of old for the salvation of his people.

The Holy Spirit was the agent of Jesus' messianic investiture that came to him by his resurrection from the dead: "established Son of God with power according to the Spirit of holiness, by his resurrection from the dead, Jesus Christ our Lord" (Romans 1:4). Jesus' resurrection was his paschal passage from death to life. And that the Spirit does for every Christian, progressively, in the Church.

12.

CHESED

The Covenant of Sinai was a two-party agreement between Yahweh and the people Israel, with an obligation to fidelity on both sides. Unfortunately, as it turned out, the fidelity was almost entirely one-sided—on Yahweh's part. As for the people of Israel, theirs was an almost unbroken record of infidelity.

Yet, because Israel's faith did arise from a covenant relationship, it possesses a unique sense of communion with God. For Israel, knowledge of God is essentially living in close relationship with God within the bonds of the Covenant. And this communion imparts a warmth and optimism to Israel's faith that is not to be found outside the Bible.

The Israelites had a special word for the loyalty and fidelity ideally shown by persons united by some bond. This bond might be that of blood relationship, or, especially, that extension of blood relationship, a covenant ritually enacted, usually in blood.

COVENANT LOYALTY

The persons thus united were said to "keep or make *chesed.*" For those related by blood *chesed* would include a fulfillment of all those obligations of mutual assistance, protection, and revenge expected of blood relations. For those united by a covenant, *chesed* indicated that attitude toward a covenant without which that covenant could not continue to exist. Loyalty and faithfulness to the terms of the covenant are its principal components. In the case of Yahweh's covenant with Israel, however, *chesed* may also have included that unconditional and unmerited love which was the basis of the covenant—that love which inspired Yahweh to form the covenant. The pardon, forbearance and mercy that Yahweh (the faithful member of the Covenant) showed to his unfaithful partner may have been meant too.

The peace and order of society in the ancient Near East depended greatly on covenant agreements. Without *chesed* there could be no peace.

But the greatest covenant of all was that between Yahweh and the people of Israel, and *chesed* came to be used predominately of that covenant. Indeed, what the Old Testament teaches us about Yahweh's *chesed* is one of the most important lessons it has to teach us. His *chesed* transcends every other by the very perfection of his being. Yahweh's steady and extraordinary persistence in continuing to love Israel, the covenanted people, in spite of Israel's insistent waywardness, is the clearest anticipation of the future salvation.

STEADFAST LOVE

The prophets especially came to realize that the Covenant could be maintained only by the persistent, determined, steadfast love of God, which transcends every other love.

The more human examples of *chesed* prepared the Chosen People for the revelation of Yahweh's transcendent love and fidelity. In Genesis we read that when Abraham became fearful that Sarah's beauty would prove a danger for himself, he said to her: "This is the *chesed* you must do me: at every place to which we come, say of me, 'He is my brother' " (Gen. 20:13).

It is difficult to find the right English word to translate *chesed* in contexts such as this. Most modern translations have "kindness" or "favor," but it seems that Abraham regarded Sarah's compliance as something more than a gratuitous favor. Abraham looked upon it as an act of loyalty and fidelity to the bonds of blood and marriage that united them and to the obligations of mutual assistance recognized as following from those bonds.

Chesed comes from a root whose primary meaning is "keenness, ardent zeal." The person who "does *chesed*" manifests his "keenness" and "zeal" for the special bond or covenant by his "steadfastness" and "loyalty." But his act may be inspired by "love" and it may appear as a "kindness" or a "mercy." All these ideas were connected with *chesed* at one time or another.

MERCY AND TRUTH

Various aspects of *chesed* (unmerited favor, loyalty, justice, mercy) are brought out in the course of one of Moses' encounters with the Lord. After he had received the two tablets of the Law on the top of Sinai, Moses remained there for forty days in communion with the Lord. Then the Lord informed Moses that the people he had brought up out of Egypt had turned aside from the "way he had commanded them," made themselves a molten calf, and were worshipping it. But after punishment the Lord relented and instructed Moses to bring two new tablets to the top of the mountain. For as the Lord proclaims, he is "a God, merciful and gracious, slow to anger, and abounding in *chesed* and faithfulness (*emeth*), keeping *chesed* for thousands, forgiving iniquity and transgression and sin, but who leaves nothing unpunished, visiting the iniquity of the fathers upon the children and the children's children, to the third and the fourth generation" (Ex. 34:6–7).

The most frequently used synonym for *chesed* is "truth" (*emeth*). In Hebrew the word is connected with a stem meaning "to steady," "to hold out." Yahweh is the God of true faithfulness, the reliable God. This is a theme that appears in all parts of the Old Testament. His followers must act in the same way.

When Joshua sent spies into Canaan, they went to the house of Rahab the harlot, and lodged there. The king of Jericho was informed of their presence, but Rahab hid them and threw their pursuers off the scent. Then she came to the spies and asked that they show her the same loyalty she had shown them. "Now then, swear to me by the LORD that as I have shown *chesed* to you, you will show *chesed* to my father's house, and that you will give me truth (*emeth*)" (Joshua 2:12).

When David was being harried by the distracted Saul, he was greatly aided by Jonathan, with whom he had formed a special covenant. And when David had won full control of the country, he asked: "Is there still any one left of the house of Saul, that I may show him *chesed* for Jonathan's sake?" (2 Sam. 9:1).

The book of Ruth, a reaction against the exclusivism of later Judaism, shows that *chesed* could be observed by a Gentile woman, the Moabitess Ruth. When Ruth goes and lies down at Boaz' feet, Boaz saw clearly that she was not inspired by a love that "goes after young men" (v.10), but by the fidelity of one who having once joined herself to a family, wishes never to leave it. It is this kind of loyalty that excites Boaz' admiration. "May you be blessed by the LORD, my daughter; you have made this last *chesed* greater than the first, in that you have not gone after young men, whether poor or rich" (Ruth 3:10).

Neither "kindness" nor "love" would be an adequate translation. The "love" celebrated in the book of Ruth is not the intoxicating passion of the Song of Songs. This is fidelity given for better or worse. This deep, unshakable attachment of a loyal heart is the perfection of human *chesed*.

THE JUST GOD

The human and the divine *chesed* are closely related. Yahweh is not only holy in the sense of "other," one whose presence might be dangerous, he is also "just," and by his very nature he demands right conduct from his worshipers and will be satisfied with nothing less. Anything else (sin) is a rebellion against him, an act of disloyalty, a shattering of *chesed*.

Furthermore, God's justice shows a deep-seated and fundamental bias in favor of the poor and the downtrodden, who have no helper but him. This was uniquely expressed in the deliverance of his own people from their Egyptian oppression, and all his followers must reflect this character. Both Israel's unfaithfulness to the Lord and injustice to their fellow men are a violation of *chesed*.

As time passed, Israel came to an ever better knowledge

of Yahweh's nature. But this only served to emphasize the great contrast between the firm, unfailing *chesed* of God and the fitful faithfulness of Israel. And since the prophets were sent primarily to proclaim the Lord's judgment on contemporary events, and especially, the conduct of the Chosen People, they could not help but dwell on this contrast.

UNFAITHFUL WIFE

Hosea's marriage experience taught him what *chesed* must mean to Yahweh. His own attitude toward Gomer, his wayward wife, taught him that the Lord's *chesed* meant his unshakable determination to be true to his share of the covenant obligation whatever the people Israel did on their part. Hosea's love for Gomer was so strong that not all her adulteries could destroy his loyalty to the special bonds that united them. And Hosea realized that Yahweh's love for Israel was at least as sure and strong as his own love for his wife.

Hosea made his marriage experience an allegory of the relations of Yahweh and Israel. Like Hosea's marriage with Gomer, Yahweh's covenant with Israel met with little else but unfaithfulness and betrayed loyalty. Speaking of his bride, Yahweh laments:

> *What shall I do with you, O Ephraim?*
> *What shall I do with you, O Judah?*
> *Your* chesed *is like a morning cloud,*
> *like the dew that goes early away.*
> *Hosea 6:4*

THE REMNANT

The better the Israelites came to understand the Lord's nature the better they understood the unfailing nature of his covenant loyalty. Knowing this, many Israelites went on to the erroneous conclusion that they had a hold on Yahweh. The pagans believed that a god could not exist without a people, and that he must in the last resort rescue his people for his own credit's sake. The Israelites had never sufficiently freed themselves from that way of thinking.

Amos and all the prophets after him remind the people that Yahweh existed before Israel and the Covenant. He freely chose Israel. His love may be so loyal and unswerving that he will never utterly reject his people and abandon the covenant, yet justice is his very nature, and he will not let his peoples' crimes go unpunished. Yahweh will punish these crimes the more severely, precisely because his people are bound to him by covenant.

> *You only have I known of all the families of the earth;*
> *therefore I will visit you for all your iniquities.*
>
> *Amos 3:2*

On the one hand the sins of Yahweh's people must meet with a just and terrible retribution. On the other hand, it is equally sure that Yahweh's *chesed* for his people would never let them go. The dilemma is solved in the doctrine of the Remnant. Some small portion of the people will always survive the disasters which are the consequence of their sins. When the destruction comes, says Amos: "As the shepherd saves from the mouth of the lion two legs, or a piece of an ear, so shall the people of Israel who dwell in Samaria be saved, with the corner of a couch and part of a bed" (Amos 3:12).

Amos was primarily interested in describing the magnitude of the destruction; in spite of this something survives, even for Amos.

NEW HEART

It remained for the later prophets, Jeremiah and Ezekiel, to solve, radically, the dilemma of Yahweh's justice and his unfailing love. Since Yahweh will forego neither his loving fidelity nor his justice, then Israel must change and provide the opportunity for the exercise of the Lord's unswerving love. Israel must repent. God's constant love will not be thwarted. His sure, unswerving love will find a way by which even stubborn, unrepentant Israel can turn. Yahweh will put a new spirit in his people's heart: he will sign a New Covenant with them. "Behold, the days are coming, says the LORD, when I will make a new covenant with the house of Israel and the house of Judah . . . I will put my law within them, and I will write it upon their hearts" (Jer. 31:31, 33).

This prophecy made a deeper impression on later prophetic tradition than anything else Jeremiah said, and eventually was to give the name to the canon of Christian writings. New Testament means New Covenant.

KINGDOM OF PRIESTS

During the Babylonian Exile, the Jewish faith, torn from its historical setting, was in danger of being drowned in the sea of pagan Babylonian culture. That it preserved its identity is due in large measure to the activity of the "teaching priests" who guided the people in the study of their Law and traditions.

Since the time of David the covenant community had been politically organized as a kingdom, ideally united under a Davidic king. Following the lead of the prophet Ezekiel, however, the teaching priests offered a different view of the covenant community. When they looked to the future they saw a community of a new covenant in which the political aspect was less pronounced and the influence of the priest was greatly increased. The Chosen People were to be less a nation than a *church,* a worshipping community, a "kingdom of priests," an ecclesiastical community presided over by a priestly hierarchy.

But the only way to insure this was to keep the covenant people separated from all other nations. Consequently we find the teaching priests stressing those things that distinguished Jew from Gentile (circumcision, Sabbath observance, "kosher" or permitted foods). And when the Jews returned to Palestine the Law came to be dominated by the idea of "separation" and great store was set by "blood purity."

LEGALISM

Perhaps Israel's unique faith could not have been preserved at all if the teaching priests had not adopted the attitudes they did. Unfortunately, however, the measure they did take was not without its risks. The earlier versions of the Mosaic traditions had regarded Yahweh's relation with the Chosen People as a real engagement between God and man in the affairs of everyday life; as an event that happens between God and man. The priestly version of Yahweh's revelation lacks this dramatic, dynamic character. The teaching priests regarded revelation not as an engagement or a dialogue between God and man but as something objectively given, to the neglect of man as the recipient. And when revelation is viewed in this way *chesed* is no longer loving loyalty to a person, with whom one had made a covenant. *Chesed* becomes compliance with the injunctions of a mere law and faith becomes assent to what is written in a book.

The term *chasid* now comes into use to designate the man who is scrupulously faithful to the strictness of the laws and regulations as enforced by the priestly leaders. The resistance movement to the Greek persecutors was led by a sect called the Hasidim, the forerunners of the later Pharisees. It was of them that Jesus was to say: "Woe to you, scribes and Pharisees, hypocrites! for you tithe mint and dill and cummin, and have neglected the weightier matters of the law, justice (*michpat*) and mercy (*chesed*) and faith (*emeth*)" (Matthew 23:23).

Scrupulous compliance with the letter became so important in their minds that they no longer asked themselves if their thoughts, or even their actions, were in conformity with the nature of the God they worshipped. It was because by their prescriptions they had destroyed *chesed* that Jesus was so severe with them. "Blind fools, whitewashed tombs, serpents, brood of vipers" were some of the names he applied to them.

JUSTICE OF GOD

Jesus, the New Moses, established the New Covenant in his own blood, the perfect fulfillment of the Old. It goes without saying that his New Covenant cannot be without a new *chesed,* surpassing the pale shadow of the old covenant to the same degree that the divine messiah surpasses Old Testament expectation. It is found in the interchange of *faith* that unites God and man in a personal exchange. The Gospel, the Good News of Salvation, "is the power of God to bring about salvation for everyone that has faith . . . for in it the justice of God is revealed" (Rom. 1:16).

"Justice" was one of the most frequently used synonyms for *chesed* in the Old Testament. And only the ideal of *chesed,* elevated to the supernatural order, is sufficiently rich in meaning and reality to express all that St. Paul had in mind when he spoke of this manifestation of the "justice of God."

Man's return to God is the exclusive work of God. God initiates the return and carries it out. But since this is a return of love, man must participate by an act of his liberty. This is the act of faith—a completely free and fully human act, but one by which man attests his radical dependence on God since he sees by a light that comes from God. Faith, itself a gift from God, is a submission, man's consent to the work that God does in him. An adhesion of the intellect to truths, faith is even more the adhesion of our entire person to the Person of God.

GRACE OF GOD

In the Greek translation of the Old Testament (Septuagint), *chesed* was most frequently translated "mercy" (*eleos*), but the idea of God's loyalty to the covenant was also implied and *eleos* may be translated as "covenant-love." Here "mercy" especially represents God's pitying regard for man as weak and helpless. The New Testament, on the other hand, prefers the word "grace" (*charis*) to express the same idea, meaning primarily God's forgiving love towards man as a sinner.

While "grace" as a word and a concept was the common property of the Church, it was St. Paul who most thoroughly developed the theme of grace. For him the Gospel is the "gospel of the grace of God" (Acts 20:24). Faced with the necessity of preserving the Gospel against Judaizers, St. Paul develops the basic contrast: grace and works, or grace and Law. Grace is an absolutely free and unearned *gift,* and the merest hint of salvation by works destroys the Gospel of Grace. "For by *grace* you have been saved through faith. This salvation does not come from you; a gift of God—it does not come from works, lest any man should be able to boast" (Eph. 2:8–9). *Chesed* is brought to full flowering in the communion of the New Covenant. God's objective, saving activity in Jesus Christ through the Holy Spirit (grace) finds its compliment in our subjective response (faith) which is itself a gift.

St. Paul's own calling to life in Christ is the clearest proof of this. Christ called him to his service: "me, formerly a blasphemer, a persecutor, and insulter. But I received *mercy* because I had acted ignorantly, in unbelief; and the *grace* of our Lord superabounded in me with the *faith* and charity that are in Christ Jesus. This saying is sure and worthy of full acceptance: Christ Jesus came into the world to save sinners, of whom I am, myself, the foremost. And if I received *mercy,* it was for this purpose, that in me, as the foremost, Jesus Christ might display his perfect *patience,* making me an example for those who must believe in him for the attainment of life everlasting" (1 Tim. 1:13–16).

A similar contrast is found in the prologue to St. John's Gospel—practically the only place the word "grace" is used in Johannine literature. The Incarnate Word is declared to be "full of *grace* and *truth*" (1:16) and he is contrasted with Moses: "The Law was given through Moses: *grace* and *truth* came through Jesus Christ (1:17). Jesus is the fulness of grace and "of his fulness we have all received, and grace for grace" (1:16). The last phrase seems to mean: a grace corresponding to the grace that is in the Incarnate Word, or, a grace of the New Covenant in place of that of the Old Covenant.

Grace is given as an absolutely free and unmerited *gift,* but once it has been received it becomes a *task* for the Christian. Let no one say, St. Paul warns the Romans, that we should continue in sin that grace may abound. "If we are dead to sin, how can we continue to live in it" (6:2). Christians must produce works worthy of the gift they have received. "Be merciful, even as your Father is merciful" (Luke 6:36); "be perfect, even as your heavenly Father is perfect" (Mt. 5:48).

Works of mercy and forgiveness of injuries are the Christian's proper response to the grace and mercy he himself has received but not earned. "Be kind to one another, merciful, forgiving one another, as God has forgiven you in Christ (Eph. 4:32). An act that is pleasing to God is itself a grace (*charis*) and should express the Christian's gratitude and

157

thanksgiving (*eu-charis-tia*) for what God has done for him. Our lives should be a grateful response to the grace of our Lord Jesus Christ who, though he was rich, yet for our sake became poor, so that by his poverty we might become rich (2 Cor. 8:9).

13.

PEACE

There are a number of Hebrew words, such as "hallelujah" and "amen" that have become such a part of our language that we are no longer aware of their origin. Counting out all such words, the Hebrew word known by most people surely must be the word for "peace," *shalom.* And this is as it should be. If there is one word that sums up the Lord's promises to his people and their hopes, it is the word "peace."

As with all their hopes, the Israelites began by understanding the blessings of "peace" in quite material terms. So the Lord had to correct their hope and fulfill the promise at one and the same time. Jesus, the hope of the ages, was the promised Prince of Peace, but as he told his apostles at the Last Supper, "I do not give you peace as the world gives it" (John 14:27).

The ancient Hebrews prized peace and longed for it even before they were formed into the nation Israel and became the people of God. When they were a pastoral people, keepers of flocks and herds, we are told that they greeted one another just as Bedouins greet friends and strangers on the desert even today: *"Salaam, Salaam alleikum,"* "Peace, peace to every one of you."

TRIBAL SOLIDARITY

Today when we are glorifying our own frontier tradition, we have surely all been made aware that a certain amount of violence seems to have been an inseparable part of that life. The same could be said about the life of the Hebrew patriarchs, but to an even higher degree. Tribal organization was loose and misunderstandings rose easily, especially when the use of wells and cisterns was in question. When these conflicts were not settled peacefully, war was the result. The tribal leader would decide and all the men would have to follow.

In this environment, the existence of an isolated individual, one not attached to any tribe, was impossible. All needed the protection that only the tribe could afford. The bond of blood, by birth or adoption, that existed between members of a tribe, created a lively sense of tribal solidarity. Any injury or dishonor shown to any member was shown to the group as a whole. The group had an obligation to protect its weak and oppressed members. But the gravest of these obligations was that of blood vengeance. The blood of a relative must be avenged by the murder of the one that spilled it, or someone in his family. This law is expressed with savage violence in the Song of Lamech:

> *I have slain a man for a wound,*
> *a young man for bruise.*
> *If Cain is avenged sevenfold,*
> *truly Lamech seventy-sevenfold.*
> Gen. 4:23b–24

Lamech was a descendant of Cain who was condemned to a life in the desert. The Lord had put a mark on Cain and had said: "If any one slays Cain, vengeance shall be taken on him sevenfold" (Gen. 4:15). In these words the Lord indicated the social reason for the institution. It was meant to be a safeguard. Under the uncentralized government of the

160

patriarchs, only the threat of blood vengeance acted as a restraint on the violence of individuals and groups. But experience shows that all too often it must have had the opposite effect—touching off a chain reaction of ever-increasing violence that turned life into a nightmare. When there was no peace, every evil was abroad. Peace contained within itself every blessing.

VENGEANCE IN OLD LAW

These are the people with whom the Lord made his covenant, making them his people. But receiving the covenant was not an immediately ennobling and elevating experience for the Israelites. The Law gradually put restraints on their violence and blood vengeance. For example, the Law commanded that there be taken only "an eye for an eye, a tooth for a tooth." In other words, compensation should not exceed damages. But the Bible stories make it all too clear that the Israelites were slow to change. They waged war and took vengeance very much as did the peoples of their time—with a violence that comes somewhat as a shock to us today. Peace and all the blessings that it entailed remained a distant ideal.

When the Israelites invaded Canaan, they may have come in with the express intention of obliterating all the Canaanite population. Some later writers certainly wished they had (Deuteronomy). But they were convinced that Yahweh had apportioned them this land and they were prepared to seize it by waging war.

And thus began a tumultuous two-hundred years of conflict with Canaanite and Philistine, which must have led them

to see even more clearly the blessedness of peace and to long
for its establishment.

It is easily apparent that the Israelites thought of "peace"
in a material way at this stage of their history. But so they did
of all blessings. Purely spiritual ideas would have meant little
to them. They had not yet been given any knowledge about
reward and punishment beyond the grave.

On the other hand, *shalom* was not a negative concept for
Semites—it was more than the absence of war. The Hebrew
root (*slm*) means "totality," to be complete, perfect, unim-
paired. And this meaning is not only static but also dynamic:
shalom can mean to prosper, to be in good health. *Shalom*
is a positive concept. Fundamentally it means material and
spiritual well-being and prosperity, and applies to the individual as well as society. This well-being took on a more
precise, predominant meaning for the Chosen People in accordance with the particular circumstances of their life.

COVENANT RELATIONSHIPS

Like other peoples of a similar background, the Israelites
were keenly aware of the need for communal solidarity and
the sacredness of the obligations to which this need gave rise.
And this awareness, acquired naturally, was deepened and
broadened by their unique covenant with the Lord. More
specifically, therefore, *shalom* is harmonious community,

good relations with others, without which the person cannot grow and attain happiness. *Shalom* is enjoyed most intimately in the family and extended to others by a covenant which determines relationships and is so "a covenant of peace." For Israel *shalom* depends above all on proper relations with Yahweh to whom she was bound by the Sinai Covenant. The longer Israel lived as the Lord's Chosen People the more clearly this was perceived.

Shalom, therefore, is a comprehensive concept covering the manifold relationships of daily life, and expressing the ideal state of life in Israel. So rich in meaning was the Hebrew term *shalom* that the translators of the Greek Old Testament (Septuagint) translated it more than twenty-five different ways, until finally the Greek word "peace" (*eirene*) was settled upon. But whereas in classical Greek the term is negative, meaning absence of war, all the positive aspects of *shalom* were associated with its Greek equivalent *eirene.*

KING OF PEACE

The comprehensiveness of *shalom* is brought out in a striking way in an incident in David's life. Seized with a passion for Bathsheba and plotting to put Uriah her husband out of the way, David sent word to Joab his army commander that Uriah should be sent back from the siege of Rabbah. And when Uriah came before him David inquired: "How goes the *shalom* of Joab, and the *shalom* of the people, and the *shalom* of the war" (2 Sam. 11:7). *Shalom* here evidently means success and victory.

This comprehensiveness also makes it easier to understand how "peace" became associated with David and his descendants and thereby an important element in messianic expectations, despite the fact that David was a fighting king. The monarchy, especially under David, saved the covenant people at a time when they seemed threatened by destruction at the hands of the Philistines. And then David went on to lead Israel to the high point of her national existence. Not only did he bring her victory and prosperity but he made it possible for the Israelites to continue their existence as the covenant people, which determined their right relations with the Lord God. It seems providential that the word "peace" (*shalom*) was knit into the very name of the city David chose as his capital, Jerusalem (*Yeru-salom*). The association was strengthened by the fact that a large measure of actual peace was enjoyed during Solomon's reign.

But David's successors were not as great as their forefather, and the ideal of peace seems to recede. The kingdom was divided, due to Solomon's unrestrained taste for princely splendor and Rehoboam's insolence. The divided kingdom was ruled by princes who were for the most part unworthy.

In their quest for prosperity and power, many of these kings married pagan princesses and permitted them to practice their pagan cults in the very heart of Israel. This inevitably led to a weakening of Israel's faith, since the people were already strongly tempted by the worship of the Canaanite gods of fertility.

PEACE AND THE COVENANT

Then Yahweh sent his prophets to his people to warn them that they would not know peace as long as they were unfaithful to the Lord. The prophet Elisha went so far as to anoint Jehu, saying: "You shall strike the house of Ahab, your master, and I will avenge on Jezebel the blood of my servants the prophets, and the blood of all the servants of the LORD" (2 Kings 9:7).

As Jehu came riding in his chariot toward Jezreel where Joram lay wounded, he was spied by a watchman standing on the tower of Jezreel. Four times Joram sent out a horseman to inquire: "Is it peace, is it peace, Jehu?" Finally Jehu answered: "What peace can there be, so long as the prostitutions and the sorceries of your mother Jezebel are so many?" (2 Kings 9:22).

How can there be peace if the most important relations of all, Israel's relations with the Lord, are not right? This point is central to the message of the prophets, who from Micaiah ben Imlah to Ezekiel engage in conflict with false prophets on the question of Peace or No Peace.

Intending to lay seige to Ramoth-gilead, King Ahab "inquires first for the word of the Lord" (1 Kings 22:5). Four hundred false prophets predict success. Micaiah, son of Imlah, he shuns: "I hate him, for he never prophesies good concerning me, but evil" (v. 8). When Micaiah is consulted at the insistence of allies, the prophet pronounces the Lord's judgment on the king's pagan ways. "If you return in *shalom,* the Lord has not spoken by me" (v. 28).

Micah, a contemporary of Isaiah, places the venality of the false prophets in a glaring light. They are prophets who lead the Lord's people astray:

> *If they have something between the teeth*
> *   they proclaim: "Peace!"*
> *Against anyone who puts nothing in their mouth*
> *   they declare war!*
>
> *Micah 3:5*

The prophet Ezekiel gives expression to the same complaint (13:10). The prophets interpret the political and social turmoil of their time as the necessary judgment of God on the unfaithfulness of the covenant people. To prophesy peace in the face of this would be to pass over sin. It was only after judgment that Jeremiah could write to the exiles in Babylonia that Yahweh cherished thoughts of peace toward them (29:11).

The Deuteronomic historian (editor of the books Deuteronomy through 2 Kings) incorporates this view into his interpretation of the history of Israel. According to this view, Israel's history followed a neat pattern. "Israel's ups and downs illustrated the basic theological conviction of the Deuteronomic historian: obedience to Yahweh leads to welfare and peace; disobedience leads to hardship and defeat."[1] Israel does what is evil by forsaking Yahweh and Yahweh's anger is kindled against them and he delivers them into the power of their enemies. In their affliction, the people repent and cry out to the Lord who is moved to pity and who relents. As long as the people are faithful to the covenant there is *shalom* in the land.

A GIFT OF GOD

In this way it was made explicit that peace is a gift of God. The Lord instructs Moses that the people of Israel shall be blessed with this priestly blessing:

1. B. Anderson, *Understanding the Old Testament*, Englewood Cliffs: Prentice-Hall, 1957, p. 95.

May the Lord bless you and keep you!
May the Lord make his face shine upon you and be
  gracious to you!
May the Lord reveal his face to you and give you peace!
                                            Numbers 6:24–26

While dwelling in Shittim the people began to "play the harlot with the daughters of Moab" and these enticed the people to take part in the rites of Baal of Peor. In reward for the zeal Phinehas showed in stamping out the source of this abuse, the Lord instructs Moses: "Therefore declare this: 'I grant him my covenant of peace. There will be for him and for his descendants after him a covenant, which will assure him the priesthood in perpetuity'" (Num. 25:12–13). Psalm 29 (28) ends with the prayer:

> *May the Lord give strength to his people,*
>   *May the Lord bless his people with peace.*
>   *(v. 11).*

Peace is a gift of God which the Lord bestows on the Israelites provided they are faithful to the obligations of the covenant. As a sign of God's blessing, peace is most often associated with the grace by which God establishes or re-establishes his covenant. In this way peace becomes a synonym for *reconciliation.* Israel will be able to forget the shame of youth, we read in II Isaiah: "Your Creator will be your husband" (54:5).

> *In an overflowing of wrath, for a moment*
>   *I hid my face from you.*
> *But with everlasting* chesed *I have had pity on you. . . .*

167

> *For the mountains may depart*
>   *and the hills be shaken*
> *but my* chesed *shall not depart from you*
>   *nor my covenant of peace be shaken.*

(v. 8,10).

PEACE AND JUDGMENT

But because the Lord is just, he cannot overlook sin and therefore Israel must be punished. But beyond disaster and punishment the prophets see mercy and restoration (peace). In this way *peace* is brought into relation with *salvation*. The exile and the dispersion of Israel are God's judgment, punishing the people's sin. But in the last times peace will be restored. The Messiah will be a "Prince of Peace" (Is. 9:6); "humble and riding on an ass" (Zech. 9:19). II Isaiah announces the deliverance from Babylon as a *gospel* of peace (52:7). For

> *You shall depart in joy*
>   *and be led forth in peace.*
> *Mountains and hills before you*
>   *shall break forth in cries of joy*
>   *and all the trees of the field shall clap their hands.*

Isaiah 55:12

This final peace as a gift of God in the Age to Come is envisaged in the most exalted, poetic terms, even as a paradisal existence in which all forms of strife will have been removed. In that age "they shall beat their swords into plowshares and their spears into pruning hooks" (Is. 2:4). And from peace between men, peace spreads outward to the animal world, and, indeed, to the cosmos itself. "The wolf and the lamb shall feed together; the lion shall eat straw like the ox" (Is. 5:25).

ATONEMENT

The fall of Jerusalem and the Babylonian Exile occasioned a deepened sense of sin among the survivors (the Remnant) and this found expression in an emphasis on atonement. Atonement is the setting at one (at-one-ment), or reconciliation, of two estranged parties. The Hebrew verb rendered "to make atonement" in our English Bibles is *kipper,* from a root meaning either "to cover" or "to erase or remove." During and after the Exile the atonement value of sacrifice in Israel, propitiation of the Lord and expiation of sins, was stressed as never before. Though not perhaps unknown before the Exile, both the *hattath* (sin-offering) and the *asham* (guilt-offering) became especially important in post-exilic times.

It was rather to be expected then that the Day of Atonement (*Yom Kippur*) became the holiest day of the year for Jews in the post-exilic times. The sacrifice of Yom Kippur was a sin-offering (*hattath*) of unparalled earnestness and solemnity, offered for the high priest, his colleagues, and the people collectively. On this one day of the year the high priest took the blood of the sin-offerings through the Temple Veil into the Holy of Holies (*debir*). Lev. 16 directs that he take some of the blood and "sprinkle it with his finger on the front of the mercy-seat (*kapporeth,* "propitiatory"), and before the mercy-seat he shall sprinkle the blood with his finger seven times" (16:14). God in his mercy provided this as a means of atonement—of healing the breach of covenant relationship, restoring peace, and reuniting people and individuals with God.

Although it had roots in pre-exilic practices, Yom Kippur became important as a distinct observance in postexilic times. In each era of Israelite history festivals were created that express the preoccupations, the aspirations, and the ideals of the people of that particular period; or rather old observances and holidays were reshaped and given a new meaning and thus became new institutions. The Day of Atonement is both the result and the answer to that deepened sense of sin occasioned by the prophetic preaching concerning divine judgment and the Exile itself. In the belief that the great national disasters of the past were due to the people's sins, the Israelites strove to bring on the Messianic period of redemption by strictly and minutely guarding against all manner of sin, ritual and moral. The pollution of sin must be removed lest the Divine Presence withdraw from among them. Hence comes the importance of sacrifice in the form of sin-offerings and guilt-offerings, and the sacrifice of Yom Kippur is a sin-offering in an intensified form.

The blood sprinkled by the priest in the Holy of Holies, accompanied by the confession of sins and true repentance, was the divinely appointed means of renewing the covenant life with God, which is peace. But it was in the Suffering Servant poems of II Isaiah that the Old Testament came closest to the full reality of peace. Peace is a "healing" won for the guilty by the suffering and death of an innocent man.

> *He was wounded for our transgressions,*
> *he was bruised for our iniquities;*
> *For our peace* (shalom) *the chastisement was on him*
> *and with his stripes we are healed.*
>
> Isaiah 53:5

PEACE AND THE SWORD

The subject of peace occurs in the New Testament less frequently than one might expect after this preparation. But the reason for this is not hard to find. The Jewish hope for salvation (peace) had become closely associated with the expected appearance of the Messiah, the Lord's anointed. In Jesus' time this title had strong political overtones, so we find that Jesus neither refuses nor accepts this title unequivocally. While fully conscious that he was the perfect realization of the messianic promises of the Old Testament, he avoids and rejects explicit messianic titles. When the question of his messiahship arose, he chose to speak of the Son of Man or the Suffering Servant of the Lord.

If Jesus' office as Son of David needed to be reinterpreted, so too did his office as Prince of Peace. "Do not think that I came to bring peace on earth; I have not come to bring peace, but a sword" (Mt. 10:34). His rendering the Kingdom present leads to no easy harmony. It calls for a decision pro or con on everyone's part and this will lead to division even in the closest ties. The apostles too will announce the Kingdom as a gift to be accepted and their hearers will be judged according to their decision. "As you enter a house, wish it peace. If it is worthy, let your peace come upon it; but if it is not worthy, let your peace return to you" (Mt. 10:12–13). In his farewell message to his apostles Jesus said at the last supper:

> *I leave you peace;*
> *I give you my peace;*
> *I do not give it to you as the world gives it.*
> John 14:27

171

Jesus' peace is the messianic gift itself, redefined according to his mission. The peace he gives is *his own;* a peace of which he is author and mediator. It is not the result of human endeavor but is received in faith.

PEACE OF THE KINGDOM

Jesus revealed himself as the Messiah and the kind of Messiah he was mostly by the things that he did, especially by working miracles. And, again, the offices of Son of David and Prince of Peace merge. Jesus' miracles are signs of the Kingdom in removing disorder and creating wholeness. Jesus works a miracle of physical or spiritual healing and gives the command: "Go in peace" (Mk. 5:34; Luke 7:50).

On the eve of his death, Jesus permits a modest messianic triumph, willing to fulfill the prophetic oracles and to demonstrate the gentle and peaceful nature of his messianism. As he rode into Jerusalem on Palm Sunday, some who had seen his miracles and grasped their meaning began to sing aloud the praises of God:

> *Blessings on him who comes,*
> *him, the King, in the name of the Lord!*
> *Peace in heaven*
> *and glory in the highest heaven!*
> *Luke 19:38*

The last two lines remind us of the angel's song at the birth of the Christ child. Here men see in Jesus' coming the sign that peace has been decreed in heaven and they raise the glory of it to the highest heaven.

172

When Jesus came in sight of the city he wept over it and said: "Ah, if only you had understood, you too, in this great day, what makes for peace!" (Luke 19:42).

VICTORY OVER SIN

The perfect peace of unbroken union with the Father is dependent upon Christ's victory over the chief enemies of peace, sin and death. On the evening of his resurrection Jesus appeared in the midst of his disciples and said to them: "Peace be with you" (John 20:19). Then he showed them the marks of his passion and endowed them with the power of his own victory over sin. "Whose sins you shall forgive, they are forgiven them" (v. 23).

For II Isaiah the herald of release from the Babylonian captivity had been one "who brings glad tidings, who announces peace, who brings good news, who announces salvation, who says to Sion: 'Your God rules'" (52:7). By way of the Greek translation of the Old Testament (Septuagint), "bringing glad tidings, good news" became the origin of our word "Gospel." The Gospel is "the Good News of Salvation." The life, death, and resurrection of Christ are God's "gospel or good news of peace" for all men (Acts 10:36; Eph. 6:15).

Most of the epistles open with the salutation: "Grace to you and peace from God our Father and the Lord Jesus Christ." The greeting "peace" is a conventional Jewish usage, but in the epistles it is given deeper content by its conjunction with the grace and mercy of God. In this way it becomes an affirmation that now, in Jesus Christ, peace is granted by God to all men and that they are called to live in this peace. "Having received therefore our justification by faith, we are

173

at peace with God through our Lord Jesus Christ" (Rom. 5:1). Christ's redeeming work, justifying sinners and reconciling all things to God, is entirely contained in this word: Peace.

RECONCILIATION

The epistle to the Hebrews evokes other elements of the Old Testament revelation to express the surpassing greatness of the new reality. Referring to the ritual and sacrifice of Yom Kippur, the Day of Atonement, St. Paul writes that the justice of God has been manifested through faith in Jesus Christ, "through the ransom (*kofer*) provided in Christ Jesus, whom God put forward as a mercy-seat (*kopporeth*) by his blood, to be received by faith" (Rom. 3:24–25).

Sprinkling the mercy-seat with the blood of the sin-offering on the Day of Atonement, the high priest led the Divine Presence back into the Holy of Holies from which it had been driven by sin, and in some way re-established the Covenant which Israel's unfaithfulness had broken. In the New Israel the blood of Jesus' sacrifice established a permanent habitation of God among men and in them. The Day of Atonement is the figure, the Cross of Jesus the perfect accomplishment. Jesus enters a sanctuary "not made with hands" (9:24); "he, because he remains forever, possesses an immutable priesthood" (7:24); "now, once for all, at the end of the ages, he has manifested himself to abolish sin by his sacrifice" (9:26).

By the blood of Jesus, God reconciled mankind to himself and formed a New and Eternal Covenant with it. "The God of peace has brought up from the dead him who has become, by the blood of an everlasting covenant, the great Shepherd of the sheep, our Lord Jesus" (Heb. 13:20).

ONE NEW MAN

Writing to his converts at Ephesus, St. Paul reminds them that formerly they had been outside God's covenants and the promises that went with them, but that now they have been brought near through the shedding of Christ's blood. "He is himself our peace" (2:14). He has broken down the "dividing wall" separating Jews and Gentiles—a metaphor drawn from the Jerusalem Temple with its Court of the Gentiles and inner courts reserved to Jews. Out of the two, Christ has created "one New Man in place of the two, so making peace . . . reconciling them with God, the two of them in one Body, by the cross: in his person he has slain Emnity" (v. 15–16).

Reconciliation between man and man, abolishing even the Jewish-Gentile hostility, is a consequence of the reconciliation of man to God. Just as love of men for each other is founded upon the love which God has for them in Christ Jesus, so peace between men is founded upon the peace which God grants them in Jesus Christ.

The peace of God which is received by faith in Jesus Christ is a peace which we must manifest in our lives. The world does not yet enjoy perfect peace because the Kingdom has not yet been fully established. Yet, because the Kingdom has been brought into this Age, the members of Christ's Body must not let anything disturb the bond of peace which exists between them, at the same time realizing that there can be no peace which has not as its condition the acknowledgement and acceptance of the justice of God.

175